Shaping
the Future

To

Kelli Aceto

With respect for

Your work & wisdom —

disire best as You continue —

to shape the future of Boeing

William Belgard

12 Sep 2007

Shaping
the Future

A Dynamic Process for Creating
and Achieving Your
Company's Strategic Vision

William P. Belgard
Steven R. Rayner

⁂AMACOM

American Management Association

New York • Atlanta • Brussels • Chicago • Mexico City • San Francisco
Shanghai • Tokyo • Toronto • Washington, D.C.

Special discounts on bulk quantities of AMACOM books are available to corporations, professional associations, and other organizations. For details, contact Special Sales Department, AMACOM, a division of American Management Association, 1601 Broadway, New York, NY 10019.
Tel.: 212-903-8316.   Fax: 212-903-8083.
Web site: www.amacombooks.org

This publication is designed to provide accurate and authoritative information in regard to the subject matter covered. It is sold with the understanding that the publisher is not engaged in rendering legal, accounting, or other professional service. If legal advice or other expert assistance is required, the services of a competent professional person should be sought.

Library of Congress Cataloging-in-Publication Data

Belgard, William.
    Shaping the future : a dynamic process for creating and achieving your company's strategic vision / William P. Belgard, Steven R. Rayner.
        p.   cm.
    Includes bibliographical references and index.
    ISBN 0-8144-0777-3
    1. Organizational change.   2. Leadership.   3. Strategic planning.   4. Industrial management.   I. Rayner, Steven R.   II. Title.

HD58.8.B458 2004
658.4'012—dc22   2003025985

Printing number

10   9   8   7   6   5   4   3   2   1

To my wife, Elizabeth, and my children: Lisa, Michael, Rachel, and Sarah, and to Bob, Kate, Leeann, Kathleen, and Bette. A loving and supportive family is the greatest blessing of all.

WILLIAM P. BELGARD

For my parents,
George and Ruby Rayner,
and in memory of Thomas Keefe.

STEVEN R. RAYNER

CONTENTS

ACKNOWLEDGMENTS

This book is an outgrowth of many years of work with engaging clients, courageous executives, and exceptional associates. We were able to include only a few of the compelling stories we have had the privilege to witness. At each of these transformations there was a team of executives, internal consultants, and dedicated line managers that worked tirelessly to make the transformation happen. Here are some of these heroic people.

From Boeing Airlift and Tanker Programs, we would like to thank Don Kozlowski, David Spong, Ed Schaniel, and members of the Employee Involvement (EI) team: Del Black, Stefanie Brock, Rocky Burke, Bob Carlson, Les Covey, Mona Fowlkes, Rosie Robles-Gleason, Gary Golson, Charles Macias, Dianna Meusch, Billy Johnson, Mike Miller, Rich Nicholson, Rick Payne, Bob Summers, Jan Summers, and Mack Sutton. We are also deeply indebted to Debbie Collard for her patience and strength to see things through and her unfailing devotion to quality in everything that she does.

From Boeing Commercial Aircraft we would like to thank Scott Carson, Jim Jamieson, Jim Phillips, Jeff Peace, and Tom Som for their leadership, courage, and support. From Boeing Naval Aircraft Programs we would like to thank Pat Finneran and his team: Phil Schwab, Donna Harwood, Dave Bowman, Bob Feldmann, Regina Stroup, Ron Hancock, Ron Shelley, Ann Clark, and Bob Craighead. In war and peace they earn their wings every day.

From Boeing Learning, Education, and Development, we are deeply indebted to our friend and colleague John Eckholt, without whose support none of the Boeing work would have been possible. We would also like to thank two key members of his team, Bruce Wheeler and Chuck Welter, for their unflagging dedication and support.

From Harley-Davidson we would like to thank Benny Suggs, a former admiral who is now the "big dog" at Harley-Davidson University (HDU). His brand of leadership is value-driven and heartfelt. His love for the chrome, steel, and leather of the Harley-Davidson Motor Company is second to none, and it shows through every day. We'd also like to thank several key members of the HDU team from whom we've learned a great deal about how you run a world-class corporate university. Thanks to Bill Bailey, Dale Cone, John Gaedke, Cheri Judkins, Carrie Kane, Willie Keith, Cindy Laatch, Philippa Short, and Andy Smith.

From Solutia we would like to thank Mitch Pulwer who is both a highly effective leader and a wonderful teacher. From Mitch we learned a great deal about both developing and executing strategy—nobody does it better than him.

From Microsoft we would like to thank David Pritchard, a leader whose willingness to experiment with new ideas created a remarkable organization. His focus on results, balanced with his encouragement to try new ideas, sparked many innovations that led to his team's extraordinary performance.

From Quaker Oats, Danville, we would like to thank Steve Brunner, John Pigg, Steve Hughes, and Dwayne Hughes. Together with their team, they forged a union and management partnership that saved their business and their community. From Covenant Health we would like to thank Sam Buscetta and Susan Harwood. Although the Covenant story was too new to make this book's deadline, we expect great things from them as the process unfolds. Cliff Purington of Rockwell Collins taught us that companies really can be "built to learn." Cliff is a great teacher and friend who supported us when we really needed it, and we sincerely appreciate him. We would like to thank Greg Sisson of Puget Sound Energy, who's working to create a leadership development process that's built around many of the ideas contained in this book.

We have had the privilege to work with an outstanding group of partners, colleagues, and friends. This group of professionals brought their expertise and commitment to each transformation project, enabling us to serve our clients as we would wish to be served. We would like to thank Bruce Anderson, Brett Baumann, Marc Bridgham, Phil Bromley, Joe Burger, Susanne Eaton, Bruce Ellis, Kimball Fisher, Maureen Fisher, Michael Higgins, Tom Holt, Robert Hughes, George Kersels, Skip McDonald, Colleen Officer, Marte Pendley, Gail Petersen, Helene Roos, Allison Rose, Rhett Ward, Larry Welte, Pat Westerhouse, and Dave Zuckerman.

We owe special thanks to Jim Armstrong and Mike Hunter, who began this journey with us at Tektronix. They lent their considerable talent and creativity to all that we do. We also could not serve our clients without the support and care of the "home team." We would like to thank Oca Hoeflein, Jay Kerr, Zach Snyder, Kevin Thygersen, and Steve Thygersen for their dedicated technical support.

We owe a special debt of gratitude to Barbara Brenneman,

Melodie Eckland, and Robyn Schlabach. It is through their wisdom, strength, and grace that our organization forges on, and it is their heart for service that allows us to continue to assist others.

We would like to thank Mike Snell, our literary agent, for the support he has given us on all our book projects throughout the years. Mike's critiques are always filled with many important insights.

We would like to thank Adrienne Hickey, editorial director of AMACOM Books, for believing in this book from the beginning. Her support, guidance, and patience were greatly appreciated throughout the project.

Finally, we would like to extend a special thank-you to Stephanie Hegstad, who contributed to this book in countless ways through her research, critiques of early drafts, copyediting, and design work. Stephanie also had a knack for giving us encouragement when we needed it most.

Shaping
the Future

INTRODUCTION

Don Kozlowski, who took over Boeing's C-17 program in 1993 when it was on its deathbed, is an example of a future shaper. Due to persistent quality problems and missed delivery dates, lawsuits between the U.S. Air Force and McDonnell-Douglas had emerged, and the program to build the military transport airplane was in jeopardy. Less than a decade later, the C-17 is the pride of the Air Force's fleet, and the profit engine of Boeing's (which merged with McDonnell-Douglas in 1997) military business. David Spong, who worked with Kozlowski and later succeeded him as the head of the C-17 program, refers to this remarkable transformation as "magic." Others have called it an "act of alchemy." It is the methods and processes that turned what was once corporate lead into corporate gold that we will uncover in this book.

Recognition of the Present

Becoming a shaper of tomorrow begins with an in-depth understanding of today—the changes, the trends, and the forces affecting the business must be well known. That is why we begin this book with an examination of the emerging *megadigm*—our word for the profound changes in customer expectations that modern managers cannot ignore. These expectations are largely the result of the enormous capability we have gained from information technology. We live in an age where customization is becoming as cheap as mass production; telecommuting has redefined our concept of office space; getting increased value, while paying less, is commonplace; and the advantage of cooperating with competitors often outweighs beating them. In the digital age, the old rules don't apply.

Looking back, we see how companies such as Hewlett-Packard were utilizing just-in-time (JIT) production techniques a full decade before "JIT" and "lean" became common practices for manufacturers across North America. Procter & Gamble's Lima, Ohio, plant was utilizing a team-based management approach nearly twenty years before the term "self-directed work team" came into existence. Motorola had already achieved Six Sigma quality when many of its competitors were still discussing its implications. The same will be true in the future. What today's best are already doing is setting the stage for what will be required for survival in the future—the best practices of today are destined to become the common practices of tomorrow. So the quest for excellence begins by gaining clarity about today's trends and what some innovative companies are doing to meet them. Chapter 1 begins the journey.

Developing a New Model

Change management, as it is commonly practiced today, fails more often than it succeeds. This is a surprising revelation given the billions of dollars annually poured into corporate, government, academic, and nonprofit change initiatives. Large-scale, transformational change efforts have an even more dismal record. Our goal for this book was to develop a new approach for initiating and implementing transformational change that increases the likelihood of success.

Our transformation model—titled simply "five steps for shaping the future"—is presented in Chapter 2. It is a refinement of some long-standing and proven approaches (such as developing a clear vision of the organization's future), along with new twists (focus on a single change imperative, rather than multiple change initiatives; recognize the addictive-like qualities that create resistance to change), and original ideas (apply breakthrough thinking methods to help overcome barriers; develop a fellowship of change agents to support and sustain the effort). It was drawn from our observations of numerous successful, and unsuccessful, transformation efforts, and it represents our attempt to piece together a coherent model for executing large-scale change.

A Visualization of Tomorrow

The intelligence that created Microsoft's rise to market domination does not reside within the head of Bill Gates; rather, it exists within the collective brain trust of some 56,000 employees worldwide. In a company whose product *is* intellectual property, hiring the best and brightest cannot be a cliché; it must be a best practice. And, for the last eight years, David Pritchard is the man who has overseen what is arguably the single greatest expansion of intellectual talent by any company, university, or government anywhere in his role as the Microsoft director of recruiting. Through a unique—and radical—vision of how a staffing organization could operate, Pritchard kept pace with Microsoft's exponential growth curve, while ensuring that the sacredness of the "Microsoft hiring religion" was never compromised.

Pritchard, like the other leaders we will examine, worked with his staff to create a collective, detailed, and shared vision of what the organization was going to look like in the future. By detailed, we don't mean some grandiose vision statement, or a list of platitudes about the future; we mean a description of what technology the organization would employ, how it would be organized, who its customers would be, and the roles it would require in the future. Once this description was completed, Pritchard then consistently communicated this view of the future, and reinforced the behaviors that were required to get there.

Chapter 3 focuses on the characteristics that leaders like Pritchard, Kozlowski, and Spong displayed (including how they demonstrated grace, wisdom, and strength under pressure), how organizational values were reinforced and utilized, and their emphasis on follow-through and execution.

The Need to Focus on a Single Point of Change

Classic change management suggests we need to create a comprehensive action plan, filled with the many initiatives that would need to be implemented, in order to bridge the gap between the present and the desired future. What we have discovered in examining companies that have adopted this approach is that the number of change initiatives that are needed can be as many as ten, twenty, or sometimes a hundred or more. The greater the number of initiatives, the more the energy and focus inside the organization becomes diluted and blurred. Often, the end result is an ineffective effort, with many initiatives that are never implemented.

The alternative? Find the single, strategically critical point of change that, if we align and maintain focus on it, changes everything else in the organization. We call this single point the *strategic imperative*.

Those who study systems theory are well versed in how a single change can create system-wide consequences. Physical exercise is a simple example of the impact a single change can have on a human system: Body fat is reduced, lung capacity increased, cholesterol lowered, muscle mass increased, heart rate reduced, endorphin level heightened, self-esteem improved, and resistance to colds and flu raised. A single change impacts multiple subsystems.

Experience has demonstrated the dramatic power of focusing on a single strategic imperative, and then aligning the business systems and processes to achieve it. At Boeing's C-17 program, focusing on quality improvement led to changes that achieved such diverse outcomes as a reduction in grievances from union members; the end of adversarial customer relations; an enormous increase in sales; a near-perfect, on-time delivery record; and the Malcolm Baldrige Quality Award. At Ameritech, the strategic imperative was to reduce wait time for new DSL subscribers, but the benefits were seen across the board—from improved customer service to improved installation quality, from better internal communication to higher employee satisfaction. The right strategic imperative, as we will examine in Chapter 4, serves as the beginning point for system-wide change.

A Change Epidemic to Counter Resistance

Anyone who has been responsible for leading a change effort has felt the sense of resistance from others. Even if others conform to your changes, you can see the reluctance in their eyes and the lack-luster nature of their support—why isn't it easier for people to embrace change?

It is not the new strategy, the new design, or the new roles that cause the resistance, but rather the withdrawal from what is known. It's not so much the fear of change, but the fear of losing what is already known, well practiced, and habitual that fosters resistance.

This insight explains why some employees don't respond to a well-articulated case for change, or a dire speech describing the burning platform of despair facing the organization. For some, the withdrawal from the status quo is simply too great, regardless of the logic or rationale behind the need for change.

Such resistance can be overcome—but not by addressing it in the way that classic change management approaches have suggested. The new approach is to utilize formal and informal networks that reside within the organization to create a prochange following, and to spread the change in an epidemic-like fashion until a critical mass of supporters have caught the *prochange flu.*

In Chapter 5 we describe the many parallels between resistance and addictive behavior, and we present a new model that future shapers use to combat organization resistance to change that is based on the principles of a spreading epidemic.

A Breakthrough to Overcome Barriers

The building of a 747 super jumbo jet is astonishing to watch. The skeleton of the plane is hooked up to a giant chain at one end of an enormous hangar, then it is slowly pulled through each build sequence until it emerges as a fully configured jet at the other end of the building. This is the world's largest moving assembly line—a manufacturing approach that has revolutionized how commercial aircraft at Boeing are produced. Since implementation of the moving line (first in the 737 and 717 production lines, then in the 747), the time to produce a jet has been greatly reduced. Furthermore, costs are lower, quality is better, and delivery has improved.

When dealing with a product that is arguably among the most complex ever engineered (with literally millions of individual parts), making any change to the manufacturing process is difficult, but turning it on its ear by going from a stationary build setup to a moving assembly line requires nothing less than a breakthrough.

Breakthrough is based on a daring assumption: *If you believe that something is possible, and are firm in your commitment toward it, you will likely discover a way to achieve it.* Knowing *how* to achieve the end you seek is not critical; believing it *can* be achieved is essential.

Predictably, in any large-scale change effort, barriers will emerge. The barrier may be technical or organizational in nature, perhaps related to budget or work design, but, regardless of its origin, once it emerges, the barrier clearly stands in the way of the desired change. It is at this point that applying the philosophy of breakthrough can pay huge dividends in keeping the future on course.

Chapter 6 shows how applying the breakthrough philosophy can help overcome seemingly insurmountable barriers—just as it did within the 747 program at Boeing. Where the strategic imperative defines the single point of change, breakthrough serves as the means to break down the barriers that prevent the imperative from being achieved.

A Fellowship to Sustain Improvement

Shaping the future is not a solitary act—it requires a dedicated cadre of professionals who have the applied knowledge to most effectively support the change. Internal change agents must be involved in such things as: preparing the formulation of the strategic imperative, facilitating breakthrough events, assisting in the formation and ongoing facilitation of work design teams, working with suppliers to align their efforts to the strategic imperative, identifying connectors who can help spread the "change flu," developing and implementing communication plans, and facilitating "setback sessions" in order to get the effort back on track. The list goes on and on. Without substantial internal support from knowledgeable agents of change, the effort quickly loses momentum.

While it is easy to recognize that internal consulting capability is beneficial, developing the strong skill sets required in the future to shape methodology is a difficult process—far beyond what can be expected from traditional "train-the-trainer" sessions, or even university degree programs. What is needed is a learning by doing approach, coupled with the creation of a community of practice where change agents can continually improve and refine their methods, based on what they learn from the clients they serve. What is needed is a "fellowship of change agents."

Chapter 7 describes what is required to sustain a future-oriented, flexible organizational culture over the long haul. The chapter discusses the role of the change agent fellowship, and the mechanics for creating one.

The steps of future shaping may seem remarkably simple: Develop a grasp of the pressures and opportunities of the present; with this understanding, develop a vivid description of a desired future; identify the single, strategic imperative that must be achieved to get there; counter resistance by creating a prochange epidemic; create breakthroughs to overcome difficult technical and social barriers; and develop the internal capability to sustain the change over time. Carrying out the steps, however, presents a deep challenge.

The successful leaders we observed were not clairvoyant—for the most part they were pragmatists who saw opportunities and focused the energies of their organizations on exploiting them. They did act on a new model, though—a model that went beyond rapid response to change as the pinnacle of organization design and management excellence. They did not seek to react to tomorrow's challenges; they sought to shape them.

PART I

MANAGING IN AN ERA OF PROFOUND CHANGE

CHAPTER

THE MEGADIGM: Confronting the Six Shifts of Change

Garry Kasparov examined the position of each chess piece. His pale face conveyed disbelief, frustration, and confusion. How could he, the world's greatest chess player, lose after just nineteen moves? A stunned audience looked on as Kasparov stood, turned away from the chessboard, and walked out. It was the first chess tournament the young Azerbaijan-born man had ever lost.

At the moment of Kasparov's resignation, his opponent registered no emotion, felt no happiness for the unprecedented win, showed no remorse for how—move after move—it meticulously broke and tormented the man who was arguably the greatest chess player in a generation. Not a sound came from Kasparov's opponent except for the constant hum of its cooling fans. Deep Blue had accomplished what some thought was impossible. The IBM computer—a mere machine—had defeated the world's greatest player in the ultimate game of intellect, creativity, and strategy.[1]

During the match, Deep Blue had an enormous computational

advantage, able to examine over 200 million possible positions per second, compared to Kasparov's ability to consider about three per second. Such extraordinary information-processing capability is the essence of our digital age. Today, enormous libraries of information are a keystroke away. Our concepts of time, distance, and place have been altered through the use of e-mail and the rise of telecommuting. Our ability to gain and apply knowledge about our customers, in order to shape everything from the types of services they receive to the amount of inventory we order, has exponentially grown. Deep Blue's 1997 victory is a symbol of how far information technology has come and how it has changed us.

With these ever-expanding capabilities, information technology is helping to redefine much of what we have accepted as "truth" in the past. We are witnessing the emergence of numerous shifts that collectively create a *"megadigm"*—a set of changes so deep and profound that they fundamentally alter our accepted worldview. And nowhere are these shifts surfacing more quickly, or with greater impact, than within business, governmental, and educational institutions.

The Megadigm

Like many others, we were first introduced to the concept of a *"paradigm"* by the futurist Joel Barker.[2] Barker took the writings of Thomas Kuhn—whose pioneering book, *The Structure of Scientific Revolutions*, first described the effect of paradigms—and showed how they could explain why scientists, academics, and business leaders often fail to recognize significant innovations.[3]

Simply stated, a paradigm is a pattern that becomes commonly accepted within a field or discipline. In the extreme, the holders of an accepted paradigm will tend to dismiss, ignore, or challenge all data that runs counter to their commonly held beliefs. As Barker so eloquently points out, this explains why almost any revolutionary idea that runs counter to existing convention will encounter heavy resistance.

In our own lifetimes, we have seen innumerable paradigms broken. We have seen expensive long-distance calls become remarkably cheap (even "free" with telephony software and an Internet connection). We have gone from the belief that nearly all forms of disease could be eliminated within a generation to the current recognition that a new generation of "super bugs" has made many of our past miracle drugs nearly useless. We have changed our perception of Japanese products as cheap and poorly made to the recognition of Japan as the model for setting the standard for high-quality goods in everything from automobiles to video game software. However, these examples of paradigm shifts are minor in comparison to the mega changes sweeping through organizations today. These new "truths" can all be linked to the enormous impact that information technology has had on nearly every element of contemporary organizational life, private and public sector alike.

In this book, we will discuss the six shifts that make up this new management megadigm. For the purposes of our discussion, megadigm refers to a fundamental and pervasive shift that alters how organizations must operate and how managers must lead. These new realities set the context in which the aspiring leader must be prepared to operate (see Figure 1.1).

The shifts are so great, the disruption to "business as usual" so profound, that most companies require nothing less than a deep change across their entire organization in order to survive the effect. Many of the shifts we will describe are obvious, and have been occurring, in one form or another, for years. Others have become

FIGURE 1.1

THE EMERGING MEGADIGM

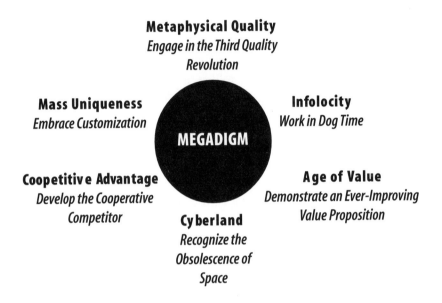

visible in only the last few years. Far more significant than each shift as an independent change, however, is their collective impact. Together, they form the new megadigm that is altering how we view such fundamental issues as quality, speed, competition, space, information, customization, globalization, and human potential. Collectively, these shifts will require an unprecedented number of organizations—large, medium, and small; profit and nonprofit; industrial and governmental—to undergo nothing less than transformational change.

Intangible Quality: Engage in the Third Quality Revolution

Our introduction to the third quality revolution occurred while we were meeting with a group of executives from NEC—the mammoth Japanese electronics firm that builds everything from semiconductors to televisions to personal computers. While talking to an executive there, we gained an insight that forced us to rethink everything we had ever known about quality.

The NEC executive looked at us carefully, and then he began to speak very slowly and deliberately to ensure that our translator got every word. What he said had nothing to do with zero defects or parts per million (or billion) calculations. He didn't utter a phrase about addressing system and process problems. There was nothing referencing Pareto charts, or statistical analysis, or quality circles. What he said didn't reflect anything we'd read from the quality gurus. He was describing a much deeper, more profound concept of what quality could mean—far beyond anything we had previously imagined.

> What we are trying to do is create products that meet the subconscious wants and needs of our customers. We want the customer, upon experiencing our products, to say, "This is exactly what I always wanted. This is what I have always needed. I cannot imagine what life was like before I had it." You see, we are seeking quality that pleases the customer in ways he never before even imagined.

What we learned in Tokyo that day was a concept we have come to call *intangible quality*. It is not what the quality movement of the early 1980s taught us, with its emphasis on producing defect-free products, or efficient and friendly service—nor is it like the quality movement of the 1990s, when the emphasis shifted toward employee empowerment and teamwork. It is a concept of quality that falls into an almost spiritual realm. It means creating a product, or providing a service, that profoundly affects the customer. It is not only defect-free, but it is exactly what the customer has always desired.

To date, the North American quality revolution has focused on the first two stages of the quality continuum. Stage one—statistical quality—emphasizes getting the product or service done right. This means documenting and standardizing processes, and then using statistical tools to ensure the product or service is conforming to specification. This stage includes ISO certifications, the introduction of lean manufacturing techniques, the creation of standardized work processes, and training in a variety of statistical and process-related tools. For many organizations, the impact on quality has been dramatic.

In stage two of the quality revolution—total involvement—the focus is on getting the entire organization to participate in the effort to assure quality. Japanese firms were among the first to utilize widespread employee participation (through quality circles) as a means to increase quality performance. Many U.S. and Canadian firms take the idea even further by deploying high-performance teams that become responsible for virtually all aspects of quality assurance, including self-inspection, process monitoring, problem solving, decision making, and work redesign. The total involvement stage also engages cross-functional teams (including marketing, engineering, manufacturing, customer service, and finance) that work together to set new product or service specifications, and then oversee the entire development process. When effectively implemented, these efforts produce enormous improvements in quality, cost, manufacturability, and positive customer acceptance.

Intangible quality represents the next stage of the quality revolution. Unlike quality as defined in stage one and stage two, intangible quality no longer focuses on improving the consistent performance of a product or service. Instead, it is customer-centric in its focus, attempting to deliver to the customer exactly what she desires. Organizations know their customers so well that every step of the development process for a new product or new service—from conception to actual delivery—attempts to tap into the customer's psyche, to solve problems the customer never before imagined could be solved. See Figure 1.2 for a summary of the three stages of the quality revolution.

The third quality revolution will dramatically impact many

FIGURE 1.2

THE QUALITY REVOLUTION

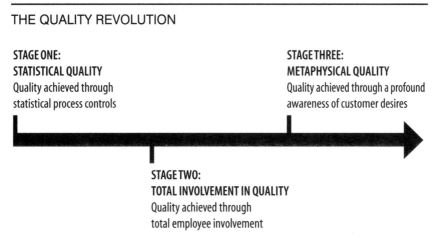

STAGE ONE:
STATISTICAL QUALITY
Quality achieved through
statistical process controls

STAGE THREE:
METAPHYSICAL QUALITY
Quality achieved through a profound
awareness of customer desires

STAGE TWO:
TOTAL INVOLVEMENT IN QUALITY
Quality achieved through
total employee involvement

businesses. Despite an investment in years of work, endless hours of training and development, the complete redesign of numerous processes, the documentation of hundreds of procedures, and millions of dollars in new technology, the occurrence of a factory achieving Six Sigma quality (and not shipping a defective product in the last five years) does not greatly differentiate it in today's marketplace. Everyone expects a defect-free, "I-turn-it-on-and-it-works-every-time" product. Quality today cannot be thought of in terms of reliability. Reliability is now the norm—nearly everyone has already achieved this consistency at a phenomenal level. The next war for superior quality will be fought at a deeper level—on the battleground of the customer's subconscious desires. See Figure 1.3 to understand the necessary building blocks for intangible quality.

The weapons that will be used in this fight haven't yet been fully defined, but information technology will obviously play a key role. In fact, a recent example of intangible quality in action is your Internet browser—a product that most of us didn't know we needed, or wanted, until we started using it. Yet it has affected us profoundly. Now, it is difficult to imagine life without reading online news, doing online research, shopping online, and using e-mail, instant messaging, or chat rooms.

One of the great competitive advantages Wal-Mart has over Kmart and Target is its ability to track what people are buying in each of its stores, then to quickly adjust its merchandise to meet the demands of a specific region, or store. While this practice doesn't exactly anticipate subconscious need, it is consistent with intangible quality, and it is, unquestionably, a factor in Wal-Mart's dramatic rise over the last twenty years.

The underpinnings of Wal-Mart's success have not gone unnoticed. And current technology now allows companies to take Wal-

FIGURE 1.3

BUILDING BLOCKS OF QUALITY

An organization cannot simply leapfrog over the first two stages in the quality continuum—they are the building blocks on which the progression to stage three ultimately stands. There are, in fact, a number of critical factors that must first be in place before any organization should even consider pursuing intangible quality:

- Strong senior management support for quality that is demonstrated in their actions

- Clearly stated quality specifications

- Standardized processes and short cycle times

- In-process quality assessment

- Quality targets and goals

- Widespread usage of problem-solving techniques

- A highly involved workforce that continually contributes improvement ideas and has the authority and responsibility to act on them

- A reward system that emphasizes quality

- Direct access to customers and/or key customer information by all levels

- Continuous training and development efforts

Mart's customer-tracking model a step further: using information about customers and their past buying habits to send them "suggestions" for items they might be interested in buying. Amazon.com begins developing a customer profile from the moment of an individual's first purchase. Each time a customer opens the Amazon Web site, the screen is dominated by product recommendations, based on what the individual has bought before. E. & J. Gallo Winery, the largest producer of wine in the world and the company responsible for nearly one-third of all the wine produced in California, sends weekly e-mails to the stores selling its wines. The e-mails provide the stores with information on which wines sold well (and which didn't), wine sales among their competitors, and estimates of the local demographic base purchasing Gallo wines. The buyer can use this information to determine the best mix of high-end and value wines to carry, and to track the impact of sales promotions. The system is so innovative and effective that it earned E. & J. Gallo a top-ten placement in *InformationWeek Magazine's* annual ranking of the best applications of information technology.[4]

Ritz-Carlton Hotels go one step father. They use a process called the Customer Loyalty Anticipation Satisfaction System (CLASS), where hotel employees record information they've gained about a customer on a "guest preference pad." This information is then keyed into a database, and it is pulled up whenever the customer makes his next reservation. Ask for a hypoallergenic pillow once, and you will find one waiting for you on all future visits, regardless of where you are in the world, or which Ritz-Carlton you visit.[5] This is intangible quality in action: knowing your customer so well that you can anticipate her needs.

Many companies are implementing customer relationship management (CRM) software to more effectively track customers. While CRM software is a critical element that can document and quickly retrieve information about customers, it alone will not enable you to provide Ritz-Carlton-type service. In fact, for most companies the customer-tracking software is probably the *least* significant aspect of providing great customer service. However, it is often the issue that gets the most attention and resources. Without a genuine customer-centric spirit within the organization (which is a result of such things as selection, training, leadership, and values) the benefit of CRM will always be greatly limited.

Apple Computer has a different slant on how to create customer loyalty—change your customers. Apple believes its Macintosh computer fundamentally changes the people that use it. According to Apple's claims (supported by some research), the ways in which the customer works and thinks are affected by the product itself.[6] The company enjoys a level of customer retention that is unprecedented in the PC industry, so there might be some truth to this claim. It would appear that many Apple users enjoy the way the product helps them to "Think Different." Is this a further example of intangible quality? Maybe—at least among Apple loyalists.

Even in the business of garbage, anticipating customer needs is critical to success. Waste Management has spent more than $400 million upgrading its information technology to achieve the goal of building customer awareness to the point "where we know more about our customers' . . . waste handling than they know about themselves."[7]

Customer loyalty has never been so crucial to sustaining a business. Yet most of the methods used to "get inside the customer's head" consist of old-school marketing relics (such as focus groups and satisfaction surveys) that simply don't go far enough. Intangible quality requires a new model of customer awareness—one that includes continuous, meaningful contact, and (we know this sounds flaky, but we really believe it's true) a spiritual connection with a customer's needs. In effect, you must become a virtual employee in your customer's organization—seeing what he sees, understanding what she understands. Then, you must use this knowledge to develop possibilities of which the customer has never before dreamed. In a world where Six Sigma is commonplace, the goal of profoundly affecting your customer is the next quality battleground.

"Infolocity": Work in Dog Time

When the family dog recently died (a beloved golden retriever and collie mix), our friend went through mental gymnastics trying to figure out the best way to explain the dog's death to his five-year-old son. He finally just looked at his son and said in a controlled tone, and without pause, "I'm afraid Sandy is dead, honey. She had a wonderful life, and she loved you very much. We will all miss Sandy; she was such a good dog."

"How did she die?" his son asked with innocence.

"From old age," he explained. "She was fourteen years old—she was a very old dog."

"But Daddy," he said, "if she was only fourteen, she couldn't be old. That's the same age as my cousin, and he's not old."

The son had a good point. The father's attempts to explain "people years" versus "dog years" got him nowhere. How come fourteen years were really like eighty-four years for the dog, but fourteen years for his cousin were—well—still just fourteen years?

As we reflected on this story (and the imperfect conversation our friend had with his son), it dawned on us that, in many facets of modern life, a year really isn't a year anymore. Increasingly, it feels like we're living in dog years.

Some have come to refer to this new time scale as Internet time, which is, roughly defined, about the same as dog time.[8] This means that every two months, an Internet year clicks by. A full six Internet years pass before the earth makes just one revolution around the sun. This concept of Internet time attempts to capture the mind-numbing speed of change that has engulfed much of the business world. It recognizes that change is occurring at a rate more akin to future shock on steroids than our traditional 365-day calendar.

More and more companies are realizing that they must adopt the Internet clock. Time to market for a new product must move from years to months; implementation of a new technology must move from months to days; critical decisions must be made not in days, but hours. The compression of time, along with the corresponding responsiveness that the organization must be able to demonstrate, is staggering.

We've all seen examples of how Internet time can fly by. E-commerce, which for all practical purposes didn't exist before 1996, is a striking example. By 2002, Internet purchases by consumers accounted for over $70 billion in the United States.[9] Now, imagine that you're a major retailer who didn't take e-commerce seriously back in 1999, and you didn't get a sales-ready Web page up and running until 2002. You're not three years behind your competitors (and millions of dollars poorer) at this point, but eighteen Internet years behind. When translated to Internet time, three years of missed trends is the old calendar equivalent of passing up an opportunity that happens once in a generation.

It's now well known that Microsoft almost missed what might be remembered as the greatest business opportunity of the 1990s. Microsoft was (at least) a dog decade behind Netscape when its now famous "Internet strategy" emerged from the corporate brain trust. Microsoft recognized that it didn't have years to respond to the explosive business and consumer interest in the Internet; it had months. The clear pathway to quickly gain market share was to build on its strengths—the Windows operating system and its application software (such as MS Word and MS Excel). The key: Make the operating system and software applications easy to integrate with the Web browser and e-mail software—something the customer would love, but clearly a daunting task from a technical standpoint. Within days, a massive reorganization began to realign the entire company around Internet readiness.

What was most remarkable about Microsoft's response was the breakneck speed with which the firm reorganized to not just compete with Netscape, but to dominate the browser market. In fact, the shift in strategy, structure, organization, and products was so fast, and the results in gaining market share so stunning, that it graphically depicts another truth about Internet time: Today's market leader may be just a dog year away from second (or third, or fourth) place.

This need to compress time has led to new and intriguing ways of doing business. Imagine a business model where no project ever stops; it merely shifts time zones. The implications? A potential 66.7 percent reduction in the time it takes to complete a project, or get a product to market. Sound intriguing? It's already happening.

The software development company Syntel was among the first firms to successfully implement the continuous workday by locating project teams in various time zones around the world. (Many other companies have since copied the model).[10] By having strong network links and common project management methodologies, work completed by the end of the day in the Santa Fe, New Mexico, office could be transferred to Mumbai, India, where the workday was just beginning. Such a strategy was used with a time-sensitive project for the State of New Mexico. A previous vendor had put the state in an enormous bind over the development of an application critical to the state's computer system. Over budget, and way behind schedule, the state called in Syntel out of desperation.

"It was like running a twenty-four-hour shop," noted Harry Beck, project manager for the state of New Mexico. Syntel's nonstop process turned the project around, and it saved the state an estimated $16 million in the first year of implementation.[11]

When Syntel opens a new office, a key consideration is the time zone in which it will be located. Completing complex projects more quickly than its competitors is the core element of Syntel's business strategy. The design team for Boeing's 7E7 program is following a similar strategy with design engineering locations scattered around the world (including Russia, Australia, the United States, and Japan). Today, no business ever needs to close. Information linkages and globalization make the continuous workday not only possible, but increasingly necessary to a business's ability to compete.

Everything happens faster today. Time, as we have historically conceptualized it, has been turned topsy-turvy. It now moves like a greyhound chasing a rabbit—and it's accelerating. Think hyperchange. Think dog years. If you're not six or seven times as fast at getting a new product out, serving your customer, or developing a new service, then chances are that you're falling behind your competition. And this trend is not isolated to high-tech. While some traditional industries such as chemical or aerospace may appear to operate in an environment more akin to horse years (roughly three times as fast, rather than six to seven times), you can be assured that their dog days are coming too. See Figure 1.4 for a final thought about the speed of change in the future.

Age of Value: Demonstrate a Great Value Proposition

As consumers, we have grown accustomed to expecting more and more for less and less. In fact, we are growing accustomed to re-

FIGURE 1.4

SINGULARITY

The speed with which dramatic, pervasive change impacts us is without precedent. Donald Schon pointed out in the 1970s that technological diffusion—the time period from the invention of a new technology to its pervasive use across society—was accelerating at a phenomenal rate. He noted that the steam engine took 150–200 years to "diffuse." The automobile took 40–50 years to become widely used. The transistor, from the point of its invention to its common usage, was just 10–15 years (see *Beyond the Stable State* (New York: W.W.Norton & Company, 1973). Taking this idea into the present, we see how change continues to accelerate—it took just three years for the Internet to hit 90 million users. Recently, some have begun talking about a point in the future where technological diffusion is instantaneous—a concept called *singularity*. While still discussed mostly in science fiction circles, the premise among the believers is that at some point within the next 20 years, technological change will occur with such rapidity that "our ability to meaningfully plan our individual futures decays into noise." (See http://members.aol.com/salaned/writings/survive.htm.)

ceiving an ever-expanding series of products and services for free. Yes, we said free. Over 200 million people use a free product every-day—the Internet browser on their computer. Sun Microsystems offers a product called StarOffice that consists of a word processor, spreadsheets, e-mail, and calendar. It's a direct competitor to Microsoft's Office software on every front—except price. The Sun version is free, beating Microsoft's retail price by $450! To compete for subscribers, nearly every cellular service will offer you a "free phone" if you sign up with them. And, talking of good deals, the speed of the latest personal computers is about 25,000 percent faster than it was in the mid-1980s, and the computers cost half as much. Welcome to the value age.

The value age is creating a new set of expectations. With nearly everyone used to getting more for less, price pressures, better service, and improved value propositions are beginning to impact nearly every industry—from consulting to computers, from chemicals to tires, from steel to airlines. For the consumer, it is a golden era; for companies, it creates a competitive field unlike any we've ever before seen.

Michael Dell showed the enormous power of the direct sales model when he started selling computers from his college dorm room. With the emergence of the Internet, this model has gained in strength. Why have a distribution system filled with middlemen when you can sell directly to the customer? The customer gets a product configured to her exact requirements that costs less money, while the manufacturer makes more money on each machine sold. This logic is beautifully simple, and it ushers in a great value proposition. IBM and Compaq were blindsided by this idea; their immense distribution system and army of retailers suddenly became a liability when matched against Dell's direct business approach.

This is the core of the new value proposition: direct linkage to the customer. Why has this become so important? If your value proposition isn't well defined in your customer's eyes, your customer will simply search the Web and find a similar product (or comparable service) for less cost. In fact, many of the current generation of search engines make it remarkably easy to comparison shop. Want the lowest airfare to Hawaii? Your search engine will find it. Better yet, type in what you're willing to pay, and challenge an airline that's hungry for business to match your price. In a very real sense, it is the customer who determines what he will pay for the product or service you provide. With the huge amount of information available, and the ease with which it can be accessed, your customer may very well know more about your competitors and the price structure in your industry than you do (see Figure 1.5).

The other side of the coin is equally as challenging. Do you

FIGURE 1.5

BEYOND THE SMILE

The customer, having done his research on the Internet, often comes in knowing far more about the product than the person trying to sell it. This is a point that is often missed in customer service training—being responsive and polite to the customer is important, but it is clearly not enough. You must have the latest information and knowledge about the product that you are selling, and the ability to effectively communicate that knowledge. If the customer perceives that the salesperson adds no value to the transaction other than operating the cash register, the customer will look elsewhere.

have an upset customer? Chances are that he will turn to the Web to vent frustrations. Instead of this customer telling nine or ten of his friends about your poor service—the old rule of thumb regarding the impact of a dissatisfied customer—he'll be telling nine or ten thousand people. Hawgeye.com is one example of this new Web-based consumerism. At the Hawgeye Web site, you'll find lots of information on Harley-Davidson dealerships across the country. Anyone who has a complaint about a dealer can e-mail comments that are then posted by this watchdog (or should we say "watch hog?") Web site. Feel like you got gouged when you bought your Softtail? Did the technician fail to fix the problem on your Sportster? You can get even by letting the world know about your experiences.

Today you must demonstrate superior value—and in most industries you must demonstrate that the value proposition gets better all the time. "More for less, more for less" is the mantra of this value-infested world. For leaders, it means getting your organization to create superior value every day.

Recognize the Obsolescence of Space

When Mitch Maddox moved into his new Dallas, Texas, house, he was elated. It was spacious inside, loaded with all the latest conveniences, including computer and cable hookups throughout—an important consideration for his new job. The location—a quiet neighborhood not far from public parks, shopping centers, and the office of his start-up firm—was ideal. The backyard was small, but nicely landscaped—a wonderful, if tiny, retreat just outside the back door. For Maddox, the house was the realization of a dream that, after months of hard work and eager anticipation, had finally come true.

Despite the home's convenient location, for the next year Mitch Maddox did not make the commute to his company's headquarters, shop at the nearby mall, visit any of the local parks, or even walk around the neighborhood. In fact, Maddox (who legally changed his name to match that of his new company—DotComGuy) did not leave the confines of his house and its tiny backyard at all. During the course of the year 2000, all of his needs—buying groceries, ordering meals, communicating with his employees, holding staff meetings, buying furniture, banking, shopping for clothes, accessing entertainment, establishing maid service, even dating—were met by surfing online or sending e-mails. With the exception of occasional visitors—the real, flesh-and-blood kind—all of his other links to the outside world were through the wire and silicon of the Internet. For one year, the former Mr. Maddox was the ultimate DotComGuy.

While his actions can be easily dismissed as a clever stunt to gain publicity for his new company (and its sponsors), DotCom-Guy's self-imposed exile also symbolizes just how different technology has made our world. Brick and mortar shops have become virtual ether in less than a generation. The biggest shopping mall in the world isn't in Tokyo, New York, or Los Angeles; it's in cyberspace. Today there are over 140 million Americans using the Internet (a new user is added to that total every two seconds). Worldwide, the number of "wired" people now exceeds 500 million, and it is expected to increase 30 percent a year for the foreseeable future.[12] Even more remarkable is the pervasiveness of the wired community in the workplace. The average Microsoft employee has nearly three personal computers and multiple e-mail accounts. To encourage computer literacy and enhance corporate communication, Ford Motor Company and Delta Airlines both offer every employee a fully equipped computer and Internet access for a small monthly fee (five dollars a month at Ford; twelve dollars a month at Delta). Increasingly, workplaces put every single employee, regardless of job level, online. If everyone in your company is communicating online, it's not a far stretch to ask the question, "Does it really matter where they do their jobs?" See Figure 1.6 for a brief discussion of some of the hazards of being "virtual."

At best, the physical work space (such as offices and meeting rooms) owned or leased by most companies is approaching obsolescence, and, at worst, it is a significant organizational liability. In the early 1990's, AT&T recognized that its sales force was spending the majority of its time in offices doing paperwork—not in face-to-face meetings with customers. To combat this trend, AT&T introduced the "virtual office"—an office not confined by physical space. In fact, the sales force was encouraged to spend as little time in its AT&T offices as it reasonably could. As a result, face time with customers significantly increased. The idea soon spread to other parts of AT&T, with resounding results. From 1991 to 1998, AT&T freed up some $550 million in cash flow—a 30 percent improvement—by eliminating offices that people didn't need, consolidating others, and reducing related overhead costs.[13]

IBM Canada went through a similar effort, eliminating nearly half of the physical space required by its staff, once housed in two great glass and steel buildings at the corporate headquarters in Markham, Ontario. Now all the IBMers are in just one building, and many don't have a "real office" in the traditional sense. When they need to be on-site in Markham, they instead work in flexi-offices—tiny cubicles with a flat surface for a laptop, a network linkage, and a telephone from which they can make calls and check voice mail. The flexi-place is shared with other flexi-workers and encompasses about one-fifth of the physical space that permanent offices would have required.

FIGURE 1.6

HAZARDS OF THE VIRTUAL OFFICE

While the virtual office has some clear advantages, there are also limitations. Face-to-face interactions cannot (nor should they be) completely eliminated. Certain types of information are best delivered face-to-face. Corrective performance feedback clearly falls into this category. Giving serious performance feedback via e-mail or the telephone has consistently been shown to be far less effective than when delivered in person. Another learning from virtual teams is that relationship building remains critically important in team settings where members rely on significant interdependencies in order to accomplish their jobs. While there are tools and techniques for strengthening the relationships of team members when physically separated, it is far more effective (and far faster in developing team cohesion) to kick off projects with several days of face-to-face meetings and team building.

On the lighter side, another negative consequence of virtual teams is higher laptop maintenance costs. A virtual IBMer sent his laptop to the shop after he had "gotten a little too much sand" into the disk drive and "spilled a piña colada on the keyboard" while on assignment in the Caribbean.

The company pursuing the vision of the virtual office more aggressively than anyone else is Sun Microsystems. Seeking to showcase the power of its iWork program, the company eliminated 7,400 conventional desks in favor of flexible workstations. For last year alone, the cost savings were $50 million (with estimates that the company will see an annual savings of $140 million a year in the near future). But, even more important, Sun is able to show its customers just how productive the virtual workplace can be, based on its own practical experiences.[14]

It is estimated that between thirty-two and forty million people telecommute in the United States alone.[15] That means nearly a quarter of U.S. workers spend at least part of their week working from home, customer or vendor sites, their hotel rooms, or, for that matter, the beach. While some jobs simply cannot be done anywhere except in the company office or the local manufacturing plant, a far greater number could be performed almost anywhere. And, as AT&T and IBM discovered, the advantages of abandoning corporate offices can be phenomenal. Decreased lease costs, overhead, equipment costs, and commute time can lead to higher employee morale, greater flexibility, and—perhaps the greatest benefit of all—more time spent in direct contact with customers, vendors, partners, and agents.

If you're hung up on getting the corner office with the big window overlooking the city, you're oblivious to what's going on around you: The traditional office is a thing of the past. If you think employees only work hard when they are under your direct supervision, you're caught up in the best management thinking of the 1950s. The physical space your company owns is expensive, outdated, and, increasingly, detrimental to productivity. Where should the people you lead be in order for them to make the greatest contribution to the organization? Chances are that it's far away from that corner office.

Coopetitive Advantage: Develop the Cooperative Competitor

When Steve Jobs announced at the 1997 Macworld Expo that Apple Computer had struck a strategic alliance with longtime archenemy Microsoft, boos and hisses erupted from the crowd of Apple faithful. Further shock and disbelief spread across the audience as Bill Gates appeared on a Big Brother–sized screen directly behind Jobs to describe the remarkable alliance the former enemies had struck. The moment was a perfect symbol of how the very meaning of competition has so profoundly changed.

Having fierce competitors with whom you also fiercely cooperate has become so widespread that it has led to the creation of a new word—*"coopetition"* (the marriage of competition plus cooperation). Coopetition, like so many other recent business trends, first appeared among high-technology companies. The origin of the bitter rift between Microsoft and Apple began over the look and feel of the brains of a computer—the operating system. Apple, the longtime standard bearer in ease of use, was dismayed at how similar Microsoft's Windows operating system was to the Mac OS. A court battle ensued, and it would have likely continued had Jobs and Gates not taken the path toward coopetition and created an alliance to benefit both companies. This was certainly not Apple's first venture into a coopetitive relationship. IBM makes a number of key components for Apple, including microprocessors and hard disk drives. IBM, along with alliance partner Motorola, has provided innovations that have enabled the Apple Macintosh to achieve unprecedented gains in processing speed—to the point it can perform many functions faster than IBM PCs. Yet, while IBM was helping to push key technologies employed in the Macintosh, it was simultaneously competing with Apple tooth and nail for computer sales and market share.

At Solutia (the corporation created in 1997, when Monsanto spun off its chemical business) a major competitor is DuPont. Yet, in order to build the market for a new category of automotive glass, Solutia solicited DuPont as their industry promotion partner. The result was the creation of the Enhanced Protective Glass Automotive Association (EPGAA)—an industry group campaigning to get the major automotive manufacturers to consider the benefits of laminated glass for side and rear windows. The laminated glass provides superior performance over traditional tempered glass. It's safer in the event of an accident (it remains in the window rather than shattering), is more protective against solar rays, is more secure (it is harder for a thief to break a window), and has better sound characteristics (less road noise enters the car). Despite the joint education and promotion efforts, one can be assured that, as more automotive companies adopt enhanced protective glass, DuPont, Solutia, and other industry players who have joined the association will be fighting hard to sell their respective lamination materials and window glass to the automobile manufacturers.

Whoever your competitors are today, they could very well be your partners tomorrow. Making sense of the competition is no longer clear-cut—there are no good guys and bad guys. You may encounter new opportunities that you couldn't even see under the old rules of competition. Contemplate this: Beating your fiercest competitor could be more detrimental to your business than collaborating with him.

It has become commonplace for two companies to engage in tenacious competitive practices and heart-warming cooperative ones at the same time. Managers may feel schizophrenic as they move from one meeting, focused on trouncing the archcompetitor, to the next, where they are actively engaged in a joint effort with that same competitor. With these dramatically different rules, managers must view business opportunities in a new light.

Mass Uniqueness: The Great Customization Wave

The technological genius of the twentieth century was mass production. From clothing to automobiles, from toys to televisions, the simplification of tasks, the standardization of components, the fractionation of production jobs, and the creation of the assembly line all led to the dramatic decline in the price of products. Where the hand-built car was accessible only to the rich, the assembly-line car was affordable to nearly everyone. Mass-produced products were cheaper, and often more reliable, than their hand-built counterparts. But mass production, the science of making the same thing over and over again, also meant less choice: If your body size wasn't quite right for a pair of jeans, or if you wanted a car in a color other than black, you were out of luck.

Advanced manufacturing techniques began to change all that. Today there truly is inexpensive customization. You can have it your way—whether it's the ingredients you want on your hamburger at Wendy's, the chip speed and RAM in your computer, the size and components in your bicycle, or the fit of your ski boots. In fact, having some level of choice has become such an expectation among consumers that the service sector has gotten into the act. Most large corporations (unless they still have dinosaurs roaming the halls) have flexible benefit packages. Most consulting firms will assure you that the problems facing your organization are unique and require a "tailored" approach. (In fact, a huge lawsuit was leveled against a consulting giant when one of their clients discovered the observations and recommendations in the report he received were virtually identical to ones the consulting firm had given to another one of its clients. The point? Provide me with a truly unique, one-of-a-kind service, or face a stiff penalty!) Any brokerage house will provide you with a survey to help you identify your investment objectives and tolerance for risk, and then produce for you a personalized asset allocation recommendation. The acceptance of "one size fits all" is gone. Today, tailoring is mandatory.

Dell Computer competes aggressively on price, but it also allows its customers to get the exact computer configuration they want. In fact, there are 16 million different possible permutations a customer can purchase (computer model, memory size, hard-drive capacity, modem type, CD-ROM, etc.).[16] If that doesn't seem like enough choice, consider Motorola's pager factory in Boynton Beach, Florida. Sales representatives out in the field electronically send in the exact specifications their customers want to the factory, where the information is translated into bar code instructions for the assembly process. Then, manufacturing begins on a single production line where any one of 29 million different possible pager configurations is produced to match the customer's order.[17]

The publishing giant McGraw-Hill now lets professors determine the contents of their college textbooks. The professor picks out the articles and chapters he wants to teach and then gives that information—along with the number of students who will be in his class—to the publisher. The one-of-a-kind book is then printed, bound, and delivered, one copy per student.

Mattel has a Web site where you can, of all things, design your own Barbie, including hair color and style, complexion, and eye color. Even companies specializing in textiles and heavy manufacturing have gotten into the act of providing inexpensive customization. It is possible to go into a Levi specialist shop and choose the style, leg type, fabric, and type of fly you want on your next pair of jeans.[18] The jeans are then ready for pickup about a week later.

Toyota has embarked on a similar campaign in Japan, where customers choose the specific model and options they want (e.g. color, seat fabric, engine, tinted glass, etc.) and receive their car a few days later. The secret is building to order, as opposed to building in batches. Under such a production system, providing your customer with exactly what she wants is no more expensive than traditional mass production. And, once customers get used to getting exactly what they want, their expectations begin to generalize. Customers assume they should always get a unique, tailored product for a reasonable price.

In his book *Being Digital,* author Nicholas Negroponte points out that in the digital world there's no reason why your tastes, friends, interests, hobbies, travel plans, daily schedule, and business deals (literally every detail about you) could not be collected and interpreted so that you aren't just receiving custom products. You're receiving reminders, insights, newscasts, and recommendations, based on everything that is known about you, your family, and your friends.[19] While this might sound Orwellian at first, imagine how popular these "smart" machines could be, as they anticipate your various needs—from recommendations for the dinner party you're planning, based on knowledge about the guests (Martha is a vegetarian, Sam loves seafood), to a reminder that your children's college fund isn't keeping up with Harvard's latest tuition increase. For a moment, imagine that your customers begin to feel it is normal to have everything they want exactly as (and when) they want it. For the manager, this phenomenon ushers in an entirely new era of complexity and challenge. Consumers increasingly assume they will receive at least some degree of customization. A tailored product or service is no longer a luxury for the rich; it is a common expectation.

The Mass Extinction of Most of Us

Sixty-five million years ago, a meteorite crashed into the earth's surface, exploding on impact like an enormous nuclear bomb. The immense heat from the blast and the accompanying shrapnel-like fire fragments set the landscape ablaze. The oxygen-rich prehistoric air fueled the firestorm as it crossed the land, incinerating every combustible material in its path. An enormous curtain of smoke rose, so dense and black that the sun could not penetrate it. In perpetual darkness, temperatures dropped and snow begin to fall. The lush, primordial jungle became covered in a shroud of white. Significant climatic change followed, and within a few thousand years, fully half of Earth's fauna and flora vanished—a dramatic mass extinction of life.

A single event, the crashing of a meteor, set up a chain reaction that ultimately rendered the dominant life forms inadequate and unable to cope with the changed environment. For today's manager, the information technology meteorite has hit the infrastructure of modern organizations. For most, it crash-landed in the early 1990s, igniting a firestorm that is sweeping across industry. Fundamental questions abound that will ultimately determine whether the ensuing climatic changes will leave your organization extinct, crippled, or thriving:

- Are you positioned to engage in the third quality revolution?
- Does your organization operate in dog time?
- Do you consistently improve the value proposition to your customer?

- Are you taking advantage of the virtual office to increase face time with customers, improve morale, increase flexibility, and lower costs?
- Are you looking for (and taking advantage of) opportunities to collaborate with your competitors in order to increase your business opportunities?
- Are you providing your customers with a tailored product or solution?

Shaping the future begins with a clear understanding of the present. The megadigm is here, yet most organizations have not yet responded. They continue their "business as usual" routine instead of carving out a distinct competitive advantage.

As we have seen throughout this chapter, the new megadigm is made up of six dramatic shifts that have altered the face of quality, value, competition, space, time, and customer solutions. Everyone wants more from large institutions (whether we're talking about corporations, public schools, government, or nonprofits).

Attempting to address each of the six shifts by establishing multiple initiatives of programs misses the very point of what's happening. You cannot establish a new quality initiative to "get inside your customer's head," as well as a new time to market initiative, value improvement initiative, reduction in office space initiative, and on and on with the hope that the combination of all these efforts will somehow make your organization more competitive. Changing a piece—or even several pieces—of the whole will not lead to sustained improvement. What organizations are facing cannot be addressed by incremental change; it requires fundamentally different systems, designs, and processes—change that dramatically alters the core architecture of how the organization operates.

For those seeking to shape the destiny of their organization, the megadigm defines a set of new, customer-driven expectations that cannot be ignored. These expectations have grown out of the amazing capabilities that information technology has created—capabilities that have created a common mind-set, based on such things as lower product cost, unique, highly tailored service that meets customer needs, and virtual offices. Much like the climatic change that led to the prehistoric mass extinction, the growing shadow of the megadigm requires many organizations to change how they do business, or face the fate of declining sales and dismal profits. Customers whose ever-heightening expectations are not met will simply seek business elsewhere.

Most organizations—whether they are in the manufacturing, service, government, or education sector—are ill-prepared to meet the challenges (or, for that matter, exploit the opportunities) of the emerging megadigm. The good news is that they can quickly overcome their lack of preparation by committing to defining a future and aligning the organization's systems and processes to achieve it. Ultimately, destiny is a matter of choice.

Notes

1. Two fascinating articles appeared in *Time* magazine shortly after the match. One was written by Garry Kasparov, and the other by IBM scientists. See "IBM Owes Mankind a Rematch," *Time,* May 26, 1997, vol. 149, n.21, p. 66. We should also note that the final word on man versus machine has not yet been written—Kasparov recently played another supercomputer, a machine called Deep Junior, to a three-to-three tie in February 2003. A German-built machine, called Deep Fritz, fared no better against world chess champion Vladimir Kramnik of Russia—that eight-game match ended in a four-to-four tie in October 2002. (See Madison J. Gray, "Kasparov Game vs.

Computer Concludes in Tie," *The Seattle Times,* February 8, 2003, p. A-13.) While the success of Deep Blue has not yet been repeated, our point remains valid: Computational power is extraordinary, and it has fundamentally changed our world.

2. Joel Barker has developed a videotape series as well as written on the topic of paradigms. His *The Business of Paradigms* videotape was very influential and helped popularize the concept of paradigms as they applied to business. (The series is distributed by Charthouse International.) Also see: Joel Arthur Barker, *Paradigms: Business of Discovering the Future* (New York: Harper Books, 1993).

3. Thomas Kuhn's influential book is now in its third edition. See Thomas S. Kuhn, *The Structure of Scientific Revolutions, Third Edition* (Chicago: University of Chicago Press, 1996).

4. Mary Hayes, "InformationWeek 500—Gallo: Technology Ferments Transformation," *InformationWeek,* September 23, 2002, pp. 102–108.

5. James Lardner, "Your Every Command," *U.S. News & World Report,* July 5, 1999, p. 44.

6. C.A. Lengnick-Hall, "Customer Contributions to Quality? A Different View of the Customer-Oriented Firm," *Academy of Management Review*, vol. 21, no. 3 (1996), pp. 791–824.

7. Paul McDougall, "Waste Hauler Trashes the Old," *Information-Week,* December 2, 2002, pp. 55–60.

8. Two meanings have emerged for the phrase "Internet time" and "Internet clock." The first meaning is how we are using the phrase here, denoting the rapid acceleration in how quickly change occurs as a result of the nearly instant access to information that the Internet provides us. In the body of the text, we equate Internet time with "dog time"—roughly meaning that time feels like it has accelerated by a factor of six. The second meaning is a more recent development, and it refers to a specific type of time measurement known as a "beat." Under the recently developed Internet time standard, our traditional twenty-four-hour day is divided into 1,000 beats (each beat lasting one minute, 24.6 seconds). In Internet time, there are no time zones, just beats that are consistent throughout the world. When

it's 450 beats in Seattle, for example, it's also 450 beats in Sydney, London, Sao Paulo, or Singapore. This standard provides the advantage of not having to translate time zones when working with teams in locations around the globe. The Swiss watch manufacturer Swatch has developed an Internet watch that measures the day in beats, but, to date, the new time concept has been more of a novelty than a useful tool.

9. United Nations Conference on Trade and Development's *E-Commerce and Development Report, 2002.* If we were to look at both the business-to-business (B2B) and business-to-consumer (B2C) sales, the number is even more staggering, and the implications even more profound. The total for e-commerce sales (when looked at from this perspective) is estimated to be $1,677.3 billion within the United States. The worldwide e-commerce market (again for both B2B and B2C combined) is estimated to be $2,293.5 billion in 2002. It's interesting to note that most e-commerce occurring today is actually comprised of B2B transactions.

10. "Growing Market for Year 2000 Services Prompts Firm to Expand Overseas Operations," *Year 2000 Wire,* August 26, 1997, Business Wire.

11. From Syntel's Web page, http://www.syntelinc.com.

12. United Nations Conference on Trade and Development's E-Commerce and Development Report, 2002.

13. Mahlon Apgar, "The Alternative Workplace: Changing Where and How People Work," *Harvard Business Review,* May 1998, p. 121.

14. Rachel Konrad, "Sun: First Come, First Seated," *The Seattle Times,* May 19, 2003.

15. Ibid.

16. "Getting Rid of Guesswork," *Business Week,* August 28, 2000, p. 142.

17. Michael W. Cox and Richard Alm, "America's Move to Mass Customization," *Consumers' Research Magazine,* June 1999, vol. 82, i.6, p. 15.

18. "Getting Rid of Guesswork," *Business Week,* August 28, 2000, p. 142.

19. Nicholas Negroponte, *Being Digital* (New York: Alfred A. Knopf, 1995).

2

A DESTINY OF CHOICE: Taking Steps that Matter

Executives who lead major corporate change efforts have a dirty little secret: *Most of their efforts are failing.* In fact, nearly three quarters of all attempted transformation efforts fail to achieve the results that were anticipated when they began. Perhaps even more shocking is that fully 31 percent of major change initiatives are canceled before they are even fully implemented—that means nearly one-third of change efforts across corporate America are simply abandoned. When one contemplates the billions of dollars and the huge resource commitment that companies dedicate in implementing information technology (IT) improvements, enterprise resource planning (ERP), material resource planning (MRP), lean manufacturing, Six Sigma, and total quality management (TQM), the failure rate is mind boggling.[1]

So, why do we see executives continuing to tout the need for large-scale change and aggressively pouring billions into initiatives that, statistically, are headed nowhere? Part of the reason, as we have seen, is that organizations are facing an entirely new mega-digm that is putting extraordinary pressures on them—pressures that require a complete reorientation of how the company operates in order for it to remain competitive. In other words, there really is not a choice. One must either attempt a significant change, or accept the inevitable decline of market share, tanking profits, and the evaporation of revenue. For many, this becomes a no-win scenario—dream big, initiate lots of changes, and ultimately fail; or, dream small, do nothing, and ultimately fail. Either way, the outcome is disaster.

But, what if there was a way to increase the odds of success? A means to move major change out of the realm of a corporate crapshoot, and into the realm of a likely success story? That's the premise of our book: It *is* possible to beat the house odds and change your organization. With a systematic approach, it is possible to *shape the future* (see Figure 2.1).

What Is Transformation?

To begin our discussion of shaping the future, a definition of what we mean when we refer to *transformation* is helpful. To transform something means to alter its nature, appearance, condition, form, or function. In a business context, transformation results in the emergence of new organization systems, processes, and culture. This description is necessarily broad, and it encompasses many types of major change, but the result of such changes is always the emergence of new operational systems, processes, and social structures that are fundamentally different than they were before the change began. The most complex form of major change is what we call *metamorphic* transformation. As its name implies, this is a dramatic

FIGURE 2.1

CHANGE GAMBLERS

> Many change efforts are a gamble, one that, historically, has not been a very good bet. A skilled craps player, using a consistent system, can reduce the casino's advantage so that his bet approaches a 50/50 chance of winning. Ironically, the bet facing many executives—only a 25 percent chance of success—is one that any seasoned gambler simply would not take.

shift, a kind of *reformation* of the organization that often leads it to new customers and markets, new technologies, and new competitors. At the other end of the spectrum, the most simplistic form of major change, is *adaptive* transformation. In such cases, the organization retains the same fundamentals (i.e. customers and markets, competitors, technologies, people), but it makes dramatic process and system improvements that lead to its competitive advantage. In both cases, transformation by our definition has occurred—systems, processes, and culture are altered—but the degree of complexity in pulling off the change is radically different. Adaptive transformation is relatively easy, since the organization is building on known strengths. Metamorphic transformation, in contrast, is extremely complex and difficult, since the organization is essentially recreating itself, emerging with a different set of capabilities. See Figure 2.2 for a summary of the four levels of transformation.

Metamorphic Transformation

In Franz Kafka's short story "The Metamorphosis," Gregor Samsa awakens from "uneasy dreams" to find himself transformed into a

FIGURE 2.2

THE TRANSFORMATION SPECTRUM

LEVEL III:
Revolutionary Transformation

Rapidly reorient what you do—develop new and different competitive strengths on an accelerated time line. Achieve breakthroughs that enable the rapid deployment of the new form, structure, leadership, and culture.

LEVEL I:
Adaptive Transformation

Do what you currently do differently—transform a weakness into a strength.

LEVEL II:
Evolutionary Transformation

Reorient what you do—develop a new and different competitive strength. Evolve toward a form and structure that will position you for competitive advantage.

LEVEL IV:
Metamorphic Transformation

Do something else entirely—re-create what you are.

gigantic insect. In this literary classic, Kafka uses Samsa's transformation as way to explore the themes of alienation, family, and power. Samsa comes to recognize that in his new, changed state the dynamics of everything around him are now different.[2]

The biological process of metamorphosis is even more remarkable than the transformation, as portrayed in Kafka's story. The metamorphosis of a caterpillar into a butterfly is truly one of nature's most fascinating processes, and one that, in many ways, is counterintuitive to what one would expect. As the caterpillar creates the chrysalis, the house in which the change occurs, one might conclude that, with each passing day, the caterpillar becomes more "butterfly-like," much in the same way that a tadpole gradually develops legs and lungs, loses its tail, and becomes more rounded and muscular until its transition into a frog is complete. Yet, this is not what happens at all. First, the chrysalis emerges from inside the caterpillar. The skin of the caterpillar literally breaks open, revealing the chrysalis. Inside the chrysalis much of what remains of the caterpillar turns into little more than dark goo. The caterpillar does not gradually become a butterfly in some step-by-step sequence, but rather much of it dissolves (in a sense returning to its biological essence) and through the process of histogenesis, it is re-formed into a butterfly.

The extraordinary process of metamorphosis is a symbol for the most extreme type of corporate transformation—change so profound that the resulting organization bears little resemblance to its former self. It deals in a fundamentally different business, has different strengths and weaknesses, and even has a different value proposition than it did before the transformation began. It is the most difficult and complex form of change to successfully lead, and its occurrence today remains exceptionally rare.

Companies that have approached metamorphic change include IBM, which over the last decade has undergone a shift from being primarily a hardware company to its position today as a provider of outsourcing, consulting services, and software design (in addition to hardware). Boeing's Aerospace Support (AS) organization is leading the way within the aerospace giant toward a similar shift, by offering a full complement of support services (such as aircraft maintenance, managing parts inventories, and pilot training). AS is demonstrating how Boeing can greatly diversify its revenue base by providing its customers with services that complement its aircraft and weapons systems.

While neither IBM nor Boeing AS fully demonstrate a true metamorphic transformation as we envision it, dramatic changes in the business environment, coupled with the emergence of the megadigm, make it likely that metamorphic transformation will be far more common in our not-too-distant future.

We will likely see more changes, such as the one under way at AT&T, as well-established companies recognize how different their future is from their storied past. AT&T is in the midst of transforming from a telecommunications company into a "software-based, Internet provider (IP)–based" company. The change is so significant, so profound, that AT&T Labs is in the midst of what chief technology and information officer Hossein Eslambolchi calls a "skill set transformation." While increasing the level of software and IP knowledge within the ranks of AT&T Labs, there has been a corresponding shift in the group's priorities and time frame. The majority of today's research—some 80 percent—is focused on ideas that can pay off in twelve to eighteen months. This is a sharp contrast to the group's old charter, where the vast majority of research was looking out at least five years or more.[3]

It is inevitable that as the competitive pressures to change increase, more dramatic modes of transformational change, like what AT&T is now experiencing, will follow. We are on the cusp of seeing waves of companies enter the chrysalis, not just for gains in market leadership, but for survival itself.

Evolutionary and Revolutionary Transformation

More commonly observed are the next two types of transformational change—what we refer to as *evolutionary* and *revolutionary* transformation. Both types, when successfully implemented, result in the organization achieving a revamped value proposition, new relationships with customers and vendors, and the emergence of a new organization culture. What contrasts the two is the speed of implementation and the extent to which performance breakthroughs are required for success. Evolutionary transformation assumes there is more time to orchestrate the various elements of the change. This puts less immediate stress on the various systems and processes in the organization. The organization can "gradually improve." Revolutionary transformation, on the other hand, assumes that implementation speed is a critical factor to the long-term success of the effort. With a limited window of opportunity, the change must be implemented quickly, often requiring significant breakthroughs in organization performance to achieve it.

Evolutionary and revolutionary transformation are analogous to a tadpole changing into the frog. The process occurs in a systematic and predictable way, and the resulting change creates a more vital creature, better positioned to survive and prosper in its environment. As in metamorphic transformation, the pathway is often filled with peril and strong resistance.

Kmart is currently attempting to navigate its way through a revolutionary transformation. As Wal-Mart flourished during the 1990s, Kmart suffered from an ineffective marketing message, lackluster customer service, and outdated technology and systems. The company was in need of a shock to its culture, according to CEO Charles Conway, who set out to remake the company on three fronts: world-class execution; customer-centric focus; and an opportunistic approach to sales and marketing. The transformation effort includes a $1.8 billion technology and supply chain makeover, better-targeted merchandise, and customer satisfaction measures to determine the impact of a new, twenty-four-hour customer service center and a host of in-store mandates to help speed customers through checkout lines and enhance their overall shopping experience. Whether or not Kmart's "inside out" approach will take it out of bankruptcy and onto the path of growth is yet to be seen, but the effort is clearly being led with revolutionary zeal.[4]

McDonnell-Douglas's C-17 Globemaster III program required a rapid, revolutionary transformation to stave off extinction. The U.S. Air Force desperately wanted this aircraft, but it was wrought with quality problems, cost overruns, and missed delivery dates. And, as we noted in the introduction, litigation had begun. The Air Force was so frustrated with the lack of response by McDonnell-Douglas that it had decided the courts were its best avenue for getting satisfaction.

The ensuing turnaround created a Malcolm Baldrige Award winner out of the former manufacturing monstrosity. As quality improved, costs dropped, and deliveries were on time. Over the next few years, the Air Force came to see the Long Beach factory as a premier example of manufacturing excellence.

In achieving the change—a transformation that even weathered the upheaval of a merger between McDonnell-Douglas and Boeing at its approximate midpoint—virtually every system and process was upgraded, or redesigned, over a six-year period. The culture that emerged was so resilient that it survived, with no negative impact on deliveries, quality, or cost, a turnover rate of nearly 70 percent—the result of Boeing shutting down nearly all of McDonnell-Douglas's commercial aircraft production in Long Beach, which caused employees from the commercial aircraft side with a longer length of service to replace fellow union workers in the C-17 program.

We will return to the story of Don Kozlowski and David Spong, the leaders who guided the C-17 program through this dramatic transition, and draw more lessons from their experience in later chapters. Their story is a profound example of shaping the future in action. Today the C-17 is the pride of the U.S. Air Force fleet and a key contributor to the success of The Boeing Company—a true example of a tadpole becoming one prince of a frog.

Adaptive Transformation

The least complex form of major change is adaptive transformation. Analogous to the chameleon that changes color to better adapt to its surrounding environment, adaptive transformation focuses on changing a single area of weakness in order to achieve a stronger competitive position. In effect, the "color" of the organization is changed, while its design and shape remain intact (i.e., the markets the organization serves, its customers, its value proposition, and its basic organization design are not altered).

Faced with immense foreign competition in the 1980s, a division of the high-tech manufacturer Tektronix introduced just-in-time (JIT) manufacturing techniques as a means to reduce excess inventory and begin moving toward a "build-to-order" system. Within a year the division, which had been losing upwards of $40 million per year, returned to profitability. Within two years the organization had become the most profitable of the company's then twenty-nine divisions.

The improvements created by implementing JIT included a build cycle that went from several weeks to less than one day and just-in-time delivery of components, which reduced inventory levels to nearly zero. Quality dramatically improved as a result of the rapid identification of errors, and morale skyrocketed as employees were trained in the JIT philosophy and taught how to identify and solve process-related problems.

The division succeeded in adapting to the price pressures of foreign competition through a change that truly transformed its manufacturing system and engineering design function, but that had little significant impact on other business functions within the division. So the breadth of the change was less pervasive across the organization—an adaptive response that turned a known weakness (the cost of manufacturing) into a strength.

In 2001 Famous Footwear found itself with huge inventories of old-style shoes, stores with outdated displays, a yearlong sales decline of 6 percent, and eroding profit margins. The ensuing transformation has focused on three areas of improvement: inventory management, store presentation, and assortment of merchandize. Old inventory has been aggressively marked down to keep it moving out, while the shelves have been restocked with the latest styles. Within the store, aisles have been widened, lighting improved, and the physical size of many stores increased by 30 percent to 40 percent in order to add new categories of shoes. The result has been impressive, with inventory already reduced by 25 percent in a year. Sales are rebounding, and margins have significantly improved.[5]

Adaptive transformation, like the examples at Tektronix and Famous Footwear, are far simpler to execute and far more likely to succeed than any of the other forms of transformation. The reason? The complexity of what is being changed is comparatively low, the likely sources of resistance are relatively small, and the required changes to infrastructure, partnerships, and technology are not so great.

Choosing the Best Path

Which form of transformation is most appropriate for the organization you lead? The answer is straightforward: Always seek the simplest pathway to the future. Do not embark on a metaphoric journey if changing the sales function (an adaptive approach) is the real key to improving your competitive position. Take the most direct, clearest, and easiest path that will enable you to achieve your ends. Always avoid complexity when simplicity will do. See Figure 2.3 for a comparison of transformational change approaches.

The Pervasive Problem

Unfortunately, for an ever-increasing number of organizations, gaining competitive advantage is not an issue of adaptation or evo-

FIGURE 2.3

A COMPARISON OF TRANSFORMATIONAL CHANGE APPROACHES

TYPE OF TRANSFORMATION	IMPACT ON CORE PROCESSES	IMPACT ON TECHNOLOGY	IMPACT ON ORGANIZATION STRUCTURE	IMPACT ON CUSTOMERS	IMPACT ON VALUE PROPOSITION	DEGREE OF COMPLEXITY IN MANAGING THE CHANGE	APPROPRIATE CHANGE MODEL
Adaptive	*Usually isolated to a single functional area (e.g., improving manufacturing performance by adopting lean manufacturing). The process(es) within the functional area may undergo significant change.*	*Typically minor changes to existing technology.*	*Organization structure remains essentially the same. Often the leaders of key positions within the organization will change.*	*The type of customer served remains unchanged. For existing customers, there is an improvement in the product and/or the delivery of the service (cost, quality, delivery, and/or service have improved in some way).*	*The core value proposition of the organization remains unchanged.*	*Relatively simple and straightforward. Improvement in the functional area undergoing the change can be achieved in less than one year. Some of the change impact will be spread to other parts of the organization as well.*	*Classic change management approaches tend to work well.*
Evolutionary	*Usually impacts multiple systems and processes including leadership, quality, safety, information, budgeting, etc.*	*While the transformation may not require a significant change in physical hardware, the manner in which existing technology is utilized may be dramatically different including new software applications and information-sharing capability.*	*The organization structure typically changes, evolving to a flatter, simpler, and more customer aligned structure over time. Typically, there are multiple personnel changes.*	*The type of customer served remains essentially the same.*	*The core value proposition of the organization may not change. While there are many short-term successes, significant improvement across the entirety of the organization can take 3–4 years or more.*	*Moderately complex, requiring the ability to overcome significant resistance.*	*Classic change management coupled with tools from the future-shaping methodology.*

(continues)

FIGURE 2.3 (Continued.)

Revolutionary	Impacts multiple systems and processes including leadership, quality, safety, information, budgeting, etc.	While the transformation may (or may not) require a significant change in physical hardware, the manner in which existing technology is utilized will almost certainly change, including new software applications, information sharing capability, and mechanism for monitoring performance improvement.	The organization structure is changed to a flatter, simpler and more customer-aligned structure. Multiple personnel changes occur.	The type of customer—and the customer's expectations—changes significantly.	A new value proposition is required for success in the future. Significant improvement across the entire organization must be achieved in 2 years or less.	Very complex, requiring the ability to overcome extreme resistance to change across the organization.	Future shaping.
Metamorphic	Fundamentally changes nearly all core processes. The only point of consistency with the past design may be core organization values.	Requires the widespread adoption and utilization of new technology.	Organization structure is completely new and utterly unrecognizable from its previous form.	The organization serves a new and different customer base than it has ever served before, or it serves existing customers in completely new ways.	The successful creation of an entirely new value proposition is required for success. Significant improvement across the entire organization must be achieved in 2 years or less.	The most complex form of transformational change, requiring the ability to overcome extreme resistance to change at all levels within the organization.	Future shaping.

lution anymore. It requires a far more dramatic, systemwide effort. Some leaders are dumbfounded by what's happening. They recognize the profound changes they face, can articulate the pervasive problem that is haunting their industry, are clear about the impact it's having on their company, but remain uncertain about what to do. How is adversity best turned into opportunity?

To begin, you must first understand the nature of the common problem within your industry, and determine how well you are currently addressing it. Often, the company that can demonstrate the ability to overcome the pervasive problem positions itself for market leadership. Here is our snapshot look at what's happening in defense, food processing, accounting, and health care, and some thoughts about the opportunities that are emerging.

Revolution in Defense

In the defense sector, two industrywide problems are hitting the major contractors at the same time. One is overcapacity. Despite recent increases in the defense budget, the combination of productivity improvements and shifts in the types of products being purchased by the Pentagon since the end of the Cold War have left huge factories and warehouses sitting idle across America. Today, there is far more manufacturing capacity in the defense sector than is currently needed, or is likely to be needed, well into the foreseeable future.

The second problem has to do with a fundamental shift in how the Pentagon now thinks about warfare in the new age of terrorism. So different is this perspective, it even has a name: "Revolution in Military Affairs," or RMA. To fulfill this new vision of military readiness, the types of products that defense contractors must provide for America's armed forces have dramatically changed. While the Cold War era was dominated by large, expensive, and often stationary weapons, the RMA era requires small, light, and maneuverable systems that can share information. The objective is to create a network-centric battlefield where every movement—from troops on the ground to helicopters in the sky to ships at sea—can be linked and operated in a coordinated manner to overwhelm the enemy. Furthermore, this capability needs to be designed so that it can be available anywhere in the world within hours of an international incident. The implications for defense contractors is revolutionary in virtually all aspects of their business—from development to manufacturing, from customer relations to service and support. The company that can establish itself as the leader in rapid deployment and network-centric solutions will be in a strong competitive position. As Secretary of Defense Donald Rumsfeld likes to remind military personnel and defense contractors, what's required for the future is nothing less than "the transformation of the Department of Defense."

Security in the Food Chain

For the food industry, a new problem has emerged: the ability to ensure the security of the food chain. In the United States, there has, to date, been only one documented terrorist act of purposeful contamination using a disease-causing pathogen—by renegade followers of the Bhagwan Shree Rajneesh. They sought to influence the outcome of an Oregon election by poisoning salad bars with salmonella.[6] However, terrorists have targeted and successfully poisoned food supplies in a number of other countries. And since the September 11, 2001, Al Qaeda attack, the possibility that food might be a future target has created a sense of uneasiness among food producers and their customers. Companies that can demonstrate a new, more comprehensive approach to the security of the food supply will almost certainly gain an increased customer base, and they will likely be in the position to set the standard that others might eventually be mandated to follow. To pull this off will require not only new processes and systems, but heightened awareness among workers to help recognize potential threats—in a phrase, a large-scale culture change of unprecedented employee vigilance.

The impact of a single incident—whether through a planned terrorist act, or a malicious employee—could destroy an entire brand (and bring an entire company down with it). While food-producing companies don't like to talk publicly about security, or the measures they are taking to ensure that the food that reaches your table is safe, we know of several companies who are adopting an approach called commitment-based security, or CBS. Commitment-based security recognizes that the final line of defense in keeping the food chain safe is made up of the employees who actually perform the work at the processing plants. What these companies are doing actually turns the traditional notion of security on its head. Instead of seeing security as the responsibility of a functional organization, they are seeing it as the responsibility of every employee. The leading companies have adopted a combination of traditional security enhancements (e.g., perimeter fencing, controlled entry, camera monitoring), while also providing training that leads to the creation of a work culture in which every employee is more attentive to potential security violations, and knows exactly what to do if a security breach is observed.

Erosion of Trust

In the accounting sector, scandal, collusion, and fraud have brought the industry to its knees. With Arthur Andersen's document-shredding debacle at Enron, followed by a slew of somewhat less publicized but equally troubling blunders by other major firms, the entire accounting industry is in a state of disarray. The firm that can establish that it doesn't collude with clients, that its practices are ethically sound and beyond reproach, and that it operates from principles of honesty and trustworthiness will come out ahead. Some firms, through TV ads showing average people "doing the right thing," are attempting to attack the issue head-on, and create the sense that they are a reputable organization. What does it take to recreate a consulting practice? Our guess is that it will require more than thirty-second television spots. The irregularities that have surfaced in the last couple of years will likely require changes in leadership, practices, standards, and culture. (The CBS approach is applicable here as well: The best way to stop ethical lapses is to provide observant employees with an avenue for reporting any irregularities that they see—without fear of reprisal.)

The firm that can establish that its practices are ethical and fair, and that its audits are thorough and unbiased, will win the business of concerned executives and nervous board members.

The Cost of Health

Like many other Americans, we cringe each year when it's time to renew our health-care coverage. The annual increases we've experienced over the last three years have averaged more than 25 percent annually, making the cost we pay for health care over twice what it was just three years ago. While our increases have been somewhat exceptional—the national average increase in employer health-care costs for 2002 was about 13 percent—many companies are finding that the only way to control their health-care costs is to go through an annual exercise of benefit reductions.[7] And for those whose companies do not provide health care, its high cost has made it a luxury item that many people simply cannot afford. Today 41.2 million

Americans do not have health insurance—that's nearly 15 percent of the country's population.[8]

Once a cottage industry of independently owned clinics, the "corporatization" of health care has, in many ways, hurt public confidence in care quality, even as the technology available to patients has improved. A difficult dilemma has emerged: How do you control costs on the one hand, and maintain high quality of care on the other? If costs are controlled by cutting staff and technology, the quality of care declines. (One study even went so far as to show a direct correlation in hospitals between cuts of registered nurses and patient deaths![9]) But, if costs are largely ignored in favor of increased staffing and state-of-the-art technology, fewer people will be able to afford health care.

It is, of course, possible to improve the quality of care, and to lower its cost to the patient. In fact, as we have seen in the manufacturing sector, improved quality is the key to lower cost. Health care is no different. The company that can demonstrate this value proposition—low-cost quality care—will own the market.

While not every industry has a pervasive problem that requires a revolutionary response, many industries—as we have seen in these examples—do. And, perhaps most important, the first company to overcome the problem that plagues their industry nearly always sets the agenda for those who follow. The spoils go to those organizations that accomplish this first.

So, if the need for complex change (revolutionary and metamorphic transformation in our model) is on the rise, even in industries as traditional as defense and food, what is the pathway to success? How do leaders move their organizations there first?

What Is Required to Shape the Future

At its core, shaping the future is about conscious choice. The future shaper must be willing to declare, in very certain terms, what the future will be, and then he must work tirelessly toward achieving it. There is no magic, or quick fixes here; shaping the future requires commitment, courage, and perseverance. See Figure 2.4 for the critical steps for shaping the future.

Many will see describing the future in the kind of detail that we advocate as a career-limiting move. The unspoken view seems to be, "If I set a vision and get it wrong, I'll probably lose my job—it's better to be safe (and employed) than to stick my neck out." However, in our experience, those who fared most poorly were the executives who did not develop such a detailed picture of the future. While boards are not fond of visionaries who fail to deliver on their promises, they are equally disenchanted with executives who miss new market opportunities due to an overly conservative posture. To shape the future requires a leader who is willing to take a stand on what the future could be, then commit to a disciplined process of execution in order to achieve it.

Establish the Future

In our research, a consistent theme emerged from the leaders with whom we spoke. It is exemplified by this quote: "When you recognize the future that you want, the place to begin your journey is obvious."

In other words, the first step to successful transformation is to develop a clear picture of what you are after. Once that's completed, the systems and processes that must be altered in order to achieve it become clear. Always start with the future in the forefront of your mind.

While most people can see the logic of this simple idea—after all, establishing a "picture of the desired future state" has been a fundamental part of change theory since the 1970s—the power of taking the next step is rarely achieved—vividly describing what the future will look like in detail, as if it has already occurred.[10]

FIGURE 2.4

FIVE STEPS TO SHAPING THE FUTURE

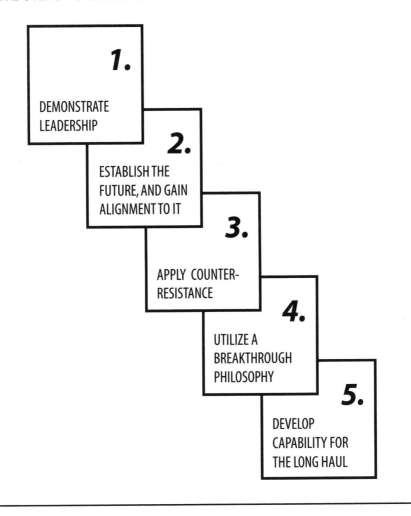

If we were to watch competitors preparing for a World Cup Ski race, we would see a combination of physical and mental preparation. The mental focus would be on visualizing every aspect of the race, running a mental movie of the future over and over again in the skier's own mind. Every turn, every gate, every point of difficulty, every opportunity to gain speed would become part of the image. This same idea can be applied to transformational change—mentally preparing the organization for the future by first visualizing that future.

The power of visualization in drawing an individual toward a specific outcome is well documented. In one fascinating study, subjects were asked to imagine that they were performing a finger exercise some twenty times each day for a four-week period. Despite the fact that all the exercises were done through visualization—there was no actual physical exercise involved—at the end of four weeks, finger strength improved by an average of 16 percent.[11]

The combination of physical practice and visualization produces superior performance among elite athletes. In fact, the combination of physical practice and visualization has been shown to produce better performance results than just physical practice alone.[12] And the use of visualization has moved beyond athletics: It is now used as a means to relieve stress, improve job performance, even to help patients fight cancer.[13] Regardless of the setting in which visualization is applied, it always requires a clear, detailed image.

Herein lies the breakdown of many change efforts—an utter lack of clarity about the end state. Sure, managers throw around flowery phrases and grandiose verbiage, but they often lack a clear picture of what the future looks like. The power of visualization comes from seeing an event in detail. For example, if you're a basketball player, simply knowing that you want to improve your free throw percentage will not lead to the performance improvement. The improvement is achieved through visualizing the bending of the knees, the coiling of the body, the bringing of the ball to the chest, the looking to the front of the rim, and all the other details leading up to the ball leaving the shooter's hand. Espousing that we're going to be a "world-class organization" isn't a vision worthy of mental pursuit unless there is more to it. Describing the future in terms of how customers will be treated differently, how departments will be integrated, how new technologies will be utilized, how teams will operate—this is the level of detail that leads to a collective sense of how a world-class organization will operate, and that serves as the starting point for the mental preparation needed to achieve it.

We refer to this as a detailed, or vivid, description of the future. To be an effective tool, the future that is described must have some *strategic* relevance, and the description of it must be written, or graphically depicted in such a way that people can understand what it will look like. In effect, the future must become tangible. It must be presented so that people can visualize the look, the sound, the feel.

Align to a Single Point

There is a natural temptation, once the vivid description is established, to generate a list of all the actions that will be required to achieve it. In our experience, this is a trap that dilutes energy, dampens motivation, and increases conflict. Once the future is clear, the question should not be, "What are all the things we need to change in order to achieve it?" Rather, one should ask, "What is the single goal—the one thing—that, if achieved, would make our vision inevitable?" We call this single goal the *strategic imperative*.

Experience has demonstrated the dramatic power of focusing on a single, strategic imperative, and then aligning the business systems and processes to achieve it. At Boeing's C-17 program, a focus on quality led to changes that were key in achieving such diverse outcomes as: significant cost savings; an enormous reduction in grievances from union members; the end of adversarial customer relations; an enormous increase in sales; a near-perfect, on-time delivery record; and, yes, significant quality improvement. At Ameritech the strategic imperative was reduction of wait time for new DSL subscribers. However, the benefits were seen across the board—from improved customer service to improved installation quality; from better internal communication to higher employee satisfaction. At Quaker Oats's Danville, Illinois, plant, "world-class productivity and waste control" became the strategic imperative leading to a production increase from 8.5 million cases of cereal a year to 12 million, while controllable costs were reduced by 50 percent. Yet, the even greater story at Quaker was the harmony that developed in the union management relations, leading *Industry Week* magazine to select the Danville operation as one of the "top ten plants in America." The right strategic imperative serves as the beginning point for systemwide change.

Systemwide change does not begin by accident. It requires a conscious effort to align the organization's various systems in a unified direction. The strategic imperative serves as the centerpiece of the transformation effort, the goal that all the other systems, processes, and technologies are aligned toward achieving. At a minimum, there must be alignment between the strategic imperative and the following (see Figure 2.5):

- Leadership
- Partnerships

FIGURE 2.5

STRATEGIC BUSINESS TRANSFORMATION

LEADERSHIP
- Demonstrate team-leader skills and visible alignment with the vision.
- Focus operational objectives on the strategic imperative.
- Achieve dramatic performance improvements through employee involvement.
- Actively remove barriers to team success.

CORE PROCESSES
- Identify and understand the core processes – those that create value by transforming raw material or data into finished products or services.
- Redesign core processes to achieve the strategic imperative.
- Operate core processes at peak levels of performance and customer satisfaction.
- Equip people to continually redesign work.

COMPELLING PARTNERSHIPS
- Fully engage customers, suppliers, unions, and other partners in achieving the strategic imperative.
- Develop shared business objectives with key partners.
- Implement innovative and seamless partnership structures.
- Develop robust relationships along the entire value chain.

STRATEGIC IMPERATIVE

A critical business goal that is highly desirable and presently out of reach, but, when accomplished, will create significant competitive advantage.

SUPPORTIVE INFRASTRUCTURE
- Focus infrastructure – finance, HR, IT, facilities, and other support organizations – on enabling and reinforcing the transformation.
- Identify and redesign support systems critical to the success of the strategic imperative.
- Integrate infrastructure efficiently into core processes.
- Develop staff roles into effective strategic resources.

FULLY EMPOWERED WORKFORCE
- Implement a team-based, high-performance environment.
- Link individual and team accomplishment to the strategic imperative.
- Tap into the full potential of the workforce to improve operations and performance.
- Create a work environment that attracts and retains the best employees.

- Workforce
- Infrastructure
- Core processes

Union and management representatives at Weyerhaeuser's Drayton Valley, Alberta, sawmill spent two intensive days planning how to align the organization to the strategic imperative of lower-cost-per-board foot of lumber produced. In working through how to better align the organization, the team discovered that each element (leadership, compelling partnerships, fully empowered workforce, etc.) needed some change in order to achieve stronger alignment to the strategic imperative. Some of the specific actions the team developed included communication of the goal; a revised set of performance measures (made highly visible); a common process for identifying and working through bottlenecks; and more direct control within work teams for making process improvements.

A well-conceived strategic imperative that is fully supported by leadership, partnerships, the workforce, infrastructure, and core processes ensures significant progress toward the vision. This is the beauty of a complex organization—achieving a single goal can have a positive impact across the entirety of the system. Therefore, rather than focus on hundreds of small actions, maintain a laser-like focus on the critical one.

Apply Counterresistance

Conventional wisdom says that if you try to change an organization, you are going to encounter resistance. Resistance is natural, it is expected, it is inevitable—or is it?

While debriefing two different large-scale change efforts of similar complexity, a startling discrepancy emerged. In the first case, every move, every decision, literally every announcement was met with skepticism, political maneuvering, and challenge. In the second case, the transition was remarkably smooth, characterized by collaboration and commitment to the new design. After analyzing what happened in each example, several conclusions became obvious to us:

1. In its most aggressive form, resistance to change resembles addictive-like behavior—rational arguments, a compelling case for change, even "proof" in the form of demonstrated results, will not necessarily curtail it;

2. The expectation of resistance often fosters even greater resistance within organizations—the mere anticipation of resistance often strengthens its presence;

3. Resistance can be countered, sometimes before it even surfaces, by applying the principles of an epidemic—in effect, creating a highly contagious, "pro-change" flu.[14]

The last point is perhaps the most important: Even in the most calcified of organization cultures, resistance can be countered, but not by addressing it, as change management approaches have historically suggested. The target is not in trying to convince those who are likely to resist the change to alter their views. Rather, the target is on getting the change message to those opinion leaders who are well enough connected to begin the spread of what can, with the right planning and guidance, become a pro-change epidemic. In other words, focus energy on getting the message into the networks where the positive message can most easily flow.

There is a remarkably simple point here: Do not try to change the resisters, but rather create the opportunity for the resisters to change themselves. While elegant in its simplicity, in execution it requires a leader who is aware of the informal communication networks within the organization, who the key influencers are, and how the message needs to be shaped so that it becomes a memorable "mind barnacle" to those who receive it. For the future shaper, this means tremendous behind-the-scenes work in gaining alignment to the change.

Adopt a Breakthrough Philosophy

Breakthrough is based on a daring supposition: If you believe that it is possible and are firm in your commitment toward it, you will likely discover the means to accomplish it. Knowing "how" to achieve the end you seek is not essential; believing it can be achieved is.

Barriers will emerge in any complex change effort. The barrier may be technical or organizational in nature, perhaps related to budget or work design, but once it emerges, it clearly stands in the way of the desired change. It is at this point that applying the philosophy of breakthrough can pay huge dividends in keeping the effort on course.

The breakthrough philosophy has several core elements that are applied when working to overcome obstacles to change. Among them is a willingness to:

- Commit, with "unbendable intent," to the breakthrough goal.
- Suspend disbelief.
- Challenge old assumptions.
- Quickly (and cheaply) test new ideas.
- View setbacks as temporary.

The benefits of applying the breakthrough philosophy to help overcome barriers to change can be enormous. Boeing's decision to create a moving 747 production line was assisted by the efforts of breakthrough teams that saw this radically different approach to building aircraft as the key to lowering costs and extending the product life of the airplane. The system, when fully implemented, will revolutionize Boeing's production process for the jumbo jet. In another application of breakthrough, a privately held food processing company achieved a $15 million cost reduction by empowering employee teams with the ability to implement process improvement. Where the strategic imperative defines the single point of focus, breakthrough serves as the tool for overcoming the barriers that prevent the imperative from being achieved.

Develop Capability for the Long Haul

The more complex the transformation, the more critical it is to have a cadre of professionals who have applied knowledge of how to most effectively support the change. Internal consultants need to be involved in such things as developing the vision of the future, preparing the formulation of the strategic imperative, facilitating breakthrough events, assisting in the formation and ongoing facilitation of work teams, working with suppliers to align their efforts to the strategic imperative, identifying areas of resistance and planning how to address them, developing and implementing communication plans, facilitating "setback sessions" in order to get the effort back on track . . . the list goes on and on. Without substantial internal support from knowledgeable change agents, the effort will lose momentum (and possibly fail).

While it is easy to recognize that such capability is beneficial, developing the right skill sets is a difficult process—far beyond what can be expected from traditional train-the-trainer sessions, or even university degree programs. What's needed is a "learning by doing" approach, coupled with the creation of a community of practice where change agents continually expand their base of applied knowledge.

The purpose of developing internal capability is threefold: (1) To assist in implementing the current transformation; (2) to develop capability that will ensure improved execution in future change efforts; and (3) to begin changing the very culture of the organization by demonstrating the value placed on individuals with strong change management skills. The individuals who help execute today's changes become the new leaders of tomorrow's efforts. It's capability development in anticipation of the future—a future that will be predictably more complex, requiring an even stronger knowledge and skill base than ever before.

The Leader Within

Shaping the future requires clarity about what tomorrow can look like; the focus and discipline to overcome widespread resistance to change; the ability to suspend disbelief long enough for needed breakthroughs to emerge; and the development of a cadre of professionals who are dedicated to support the required changes. To pull each of these steps together so that a new organizational destiny can appear requires leadership.

As we observed in this chapter's opening, most managers fail in their efforts to lead large-scale change. Fewer still actually shape a positive future for their organizations. Most perform as problem solvers—great at making improvements by reacting to and fixing the past, but poor at envisioning and creating opportunities for the future. Without clarity about where you are headed (and the resolve to do everything in your power to get there), the organization's course is set. It becomes a sailing ship that has lost the use of its rudder, floating adrift at the mercy of an uncertain sea. In order to gain control of our vessel and steer it toward the course of our own choosing, we must clearly understand what leadership means in the context of complex change.

And so we continue our journey in search of the leader within.

Notes

1. We were surprised at the number of studies that indicate most large-scale change efforts fail. The 31 percent cancellation rate cited in our opening paragraph comes from J. Johnson, "Chaos: The dollar drain of IT project failures," *Application Development Trends,* January 1995, pp. 41–47. We also found similar figures in C. Sauer, "Deciding the future of IT failures," in W. Currie and R. Galliers, editors, *Rethinking MIS* (New York: Oxford University Press, 2003); K.C. Laudon and J.P. Laudon, *Management Information Systems* (New Jersey: Prentice-Hall, 1996); proceedings from the Hay Human Resources Conference 1995; and M. Hammer and J. Champy, *Reengineering the Corporation* (Sydney: Allen and Urwin, 1994), who state, "Our unscientific estimate is that as many as 50 percent to 70 percent of the organizations that undertake a reengineering effort do not achieve the dramatic results intended" (p. 200).

2. "The Metamorphosis" by Franz Kafka can be found in many story collections, including *The Penal Colony and Other Stories* (New York: Touchstone Books, 2000).

3. Ed Gubbins, "Lessons for the Next Reality: Hossein Eslambolchi, AT&T," *Telephony,* June 2, 2003, p. 57.

4. Debbie Howell, "Kmart Overview: Conway Culture Sets In, One Change at a Time," *Dsn Retailing Today*, March 5, 2001, pp. 35, 41.

5. Matt Powell, "Staging a Comeback," *Sporting Goods Business,* February 2003, p. 48.

6. Bhagwan Shree Rajneesh cult members sought to throw a local election by sickening townspeople who were likely to vote against the Bhagwan-sponsored candidates. In all, 750 people became sick. Thankfully, none died in this bizarre 1984 biological attack.

7. The estimate in health care increases is from the Henry J. Kaiser Family Foundation. www.kff.org/content.2002/20020905a/pressre lease.pdf.

8. 2002 Census Bureau statistic.

9. Lindsey Tanner, "Nurses' Education Linked to Hospitals' Death Rates," *The Seattle Times,* September 24, 2003.

10. Perhaps the single most important book on organizational change over the last twenty-five years is the 1977 Beckhard and Harris classic, *Organizational Transitions.* See the updated edition, Richard Beckhard and Reuben T. Harris, *Organizational Transitions: Managing Complex Change, 2nd Edition* (Reading, Mass.: Addison-Wesley, 1987).

11. D. Smith, P. Holmes, D. Collines, and K. Layland, "The effect of mental practice on muscle strength and EMG activity," Proceedings of the British Psychological Society Annual Conference 6 (2), 116, 1998.

12. See G. Grouious, "Mental Practice: A Review," *Journal of Sport Behaviour,* 15, pp. 42–59, 1992; J. Predebon and S. Docker, "Free-Throw Shooting Performance as a Function of Preshot Routines," *Perceptual and Motor Skills,* August 1992, vol. 7, no. 1, p. 167.

13. Captain Chemo—a comic strip character originally created by a cancer patient at the Royal Marsden Hospital in the United Kingdom—has been turned into an interactive computer game to help patients and their families better understand cancer treatment and to help children visualize the destruction of tumors. See http://royalmarsden .org.uk/captchemo/background_info.asp.

14. We first developed this idea of how to overcome organization resistance to change after reading Malcolm Gladwell's best-selling book, *The Tipping Point.* Gladwell's work gave us a new model for think-

ing about fighting resistance by spreading a prochange message, rather than targeting resisters and attempting to change their view (as much of the classic approaches to change management emphasize). Recently, we been watching the developments occurring in the emerging field of network science, which is attempting to create models that will help predict such things as the best means to create consumer enthusiasm about a new product, or the most effective means to stop the spread of a new disease. As this field matures, we believe it is going to provide great insight into how we think about and apply change in large organizations. See Malcolm Gladwell, *The Tipping Point: How Little Things Can Make a Big Difference,* (Boston: Little, Brown and Company, 2000).

PART II

SHAPING THE FUTURE YOU CHOOSE

THE HENRY RESPONSE:
Discovering the Leader
Within

The inner struggle between self-doubt and self-confidence afflicts us all, but for those in positions of power, the fear of making a mistake, of making the wrong decision, of not being able to see the likely scenario, can lead to prolonged periods of hesitancy that begin to affect the entire organization. Hesitation to make the commitment, hesitation to spend the money, hesitation to decide until there is more data—it is all rationalized by professed logic, but it is often driven by fear. And when fear reigns in leadership, the result is stagnation throughout the organization.

We call this the *"Hamlet response,"* for at nearly every opportunity to right the wrongs that plague his kingdom, the fabled prince of Denmark chooses inaction. Shakespeare's Hamlet has plenty of information upon which to act and change the course of his future, yet from the earliest moments of the play, he resists taking direct action. Instead, he plans how to gain more information, to wait until a better time, to avoid any direct confrontation. Hamlet is not unlike many executives who, even when faced with overwhelming evidence for what needs to be done, seek additional support through data, the head nod of their boss, or the feel of a more opportune time before making a commitment. And, much like Hamlet, their tendency to hesitate often has tragic consequences.

In the mid-1990s, when Apple Computer finally decided to license its Macintosh operating system (Mac OS) to other computer manufacturers, it appeared to mark the end of a decade-long debate among company executives over the pathway for Apple's future. Apple's Mac OS, when it was first introduced in 1984, was vastly superior from both a technical and ease of use standpoint to anything that was then available. Even Bill Gates recognized that Apple could "own" the market for operating systems, simply by licensing its software to other computer manufacturers. Apple hesitated for a decade, fearful that a licensing arrangement would erode its highly profitable hardware business and make it primarily a software company.

In hindsight, the opportunity that Apple had in the 1980s was extraordinary. It's possible (many say "likely") that had the company licensed its operating systems back then, the vast majority of personal computers today would run on Apple's Mac OS, instead of Microsoft's Windows. But by the time the decision finally was made to license the operating system, the opportunity was gone—long gone. After entering into licensing agreements with several computer manufacturers in the mid-1990s, including an aggressive upstart called Power Computing, Apple found both its market share and profitability deteriorating. Not only was Apple continuing to compete against the low-cost, Windows-based PCs, but the very companies it had licensed its operating system to were offering machines that were faster, had more memory, and cost significantly less than the ones Apple built. In the end, Apple recognized that their clones weren't expanding the market share of the Mac OS; they were simply speeding Apple's decline. When Steven Jobs returned as Apple's "interim CEO," Apple purchased Power Computing, and the licensing program abruptly halted.

By initially hesitating, and then taking action long after the window of opportunity had shut, Apple was not unlike Hamlet, who finally draws his sword to kill the corrupt king he believes is hiding behind the curtains, only to find he has mistakenly killed Polonius, the father of his beloved Ophelia. The pattern of inaction, hesitation, indecisiveness, followed suddenly by an ill-conceived, unreasoned act that backfires, is the Hamlet response in a nutshell.

Hamlet vs. Henry

In many ways the Shakespearean character the least like Hamlet is King Henry V. Where Hamlet is cautious, Henry is bold. Where Hamlet avoids confrontation, Henry asserts his vision, even when faced with overwhelming odds. Where Hamlet often delays to assess the situation he faces, Henry accelerates to take advantage of newly emerging opportunities. Where Hamlet is self-absorbed with his own immediate problems, Henry is focused on a grand vision for the future. We call this action-oriented style of leadership the *Henry response.* For a comparison of the Hamlet and Henry responses, see Figure 3.1.

When confronted with facts, England's king acts decisively. He envisions England as a great power whose interests will not be denied by the French, nor the greed and corruption of his own countrymen. His desire for a grand and glorious England is far

FIGURE 3.1

THE HAMLET AND HENRY RESPONSES

HAMLET	HENRY
• Even when faced with overwhelming evidence, he seeks more information.	• When faced with credible evidence, he acts decisively.
• When presented with opportunities to take action, he hesitates.	• When presented with opportunities, he eagerly uses them to his advantage.
• When he does take action, the timing is bad, and he reacts from emotion rather than intellect.	• His actions are consistent with the grand vision that he holds.
• He alienates those closest to him by his strange behavior and self-absorption.	• He appeals to the emotions of others to support him while he maintains his focus on core principles and a vision of the future.
	• He is unafraid of ending past relationships if they violate his trust.

greater than the personal friendships of his reckless and rebellious youth.

Some may see this course as stressing action over analysis—yet this is really not the point. We believe strongly in analysis, good metrics, making rational decisions based on good information. But two forces are simultaneously changing the nature of what a rational decision is today. One is the overabundance of information. Information is like a commodity—cheap to access, and readily available. The computational power on the average desktop can slice, dice, and puree data into almost every imaginable permutation. For those who hunger for information, there is always more that can accessed. More spreadsheets can be created, and there are always new ways to crunch and recrunch, formulate and reformulate the data. At some point, the analysis becomes an obsession, not an exercise in logical decision making. The ongoing quest for information creates a paralytic effect: The mountains of data become too great to consume. Instead of bringing clarity and rationale to the decision-making process, the seemingly countless options and scenarios that emerge create noise.

The second force is the condensed nature of time. The speed of change is so fast that waiting for the additional data, before making a critical decision, may leave you an Internet decade behind your competitor. So, the key for today's leaders is to make and implement informed, rational decisions quickly. That often means basing decisions on the *minimum critical information,* as opposed to the *maximum available data* (which, in the computer age, could be literally infinite). The point is to act decisively, based on good— not all available—information.

Herein resides the first lesson: Leaders who seek to shape the future are not driven by fear, but by vision. In fact, they are able to break the pattern of what consultant and author Rhonda Britten calls the "wheel of fear."[1] They recognize that inaction is a choice that reinforces the status quo, so they have clarity about the future they seek, and they readily take action to create movement toward it. The fear of hurting one's career, alienating one's network of friends, operating counter to the company's political norms, of making a decision that will be used against you at a later point in time, are all subordinate to moving toward the vision of tomorrow. And, with this boldness comes the ability to rise above the fear that breeds hesitation.

The Disciplines of Leadership

To be a leader, capable of developing a future and transforming an organization toward achieving it, requires a set of disciplined behaviors—what we refer to as the *disciplines of leadership*. Discipline, in this context, is defined *as a learned, practiced, and applied set of leadership behaviors that increases the likelihood of achieving transformational change across a large organization.*

In all, we have identified seven disciplines of transformational leadership. They can be summarized as:

1. Demonstrate wisdom, strength, and grace.
2. Reinforce core, fundamental values.
3. Empower others—across all levels in the organization—to take action.
4. Dedicate tremendous time and energy to "overcommunicating" the future.
5. Seek short-term successes.
6. Leverage serendipity to influence direction.
7. Execute with tenacity (see Figure 3.2).

Looking at this list, one might assume recruiting trips to the planet Krypton would be necessary to find a person who daily lived and breathed each of these disciplines. Even the most gifted leaders we've worked with have a shortcoming in one (or more) of these areas. So the list is not a prerequisite for leading a transformation; instead, it defines the capabilities that increase one's chances of being successful.

We are not advocating a heroic style of leadership that relies on the charisma of a single individual to call the shots in an auto-

FIGURE 3.2
_____

THE DISCIPLINES OF TRANSFORMATIONAL LEADERSHIP

- Demonstrate wisdom, strength, and grace.

- Reinforce core, fundamental values.

- Empower others—across all levels in the organization—
  to take action.

- Dedicate tremendous time and energy to "overcommunicating"
  the future.

- Seek short-term successes.

- Leverage serendipity to influence direction.

- Execute with tenacity.

cratic manner. In fact, we believe quite the opposite to be true. A more democratic, shared leadership model is far more effective over the long haul. (Further, this position is backed by both empirical and anecdotal evidence—the emphasis that corporate boards put on finding the charismatic, superstar leader rarely pays off. More often than not, this emphasis is detrimental to long-term performance.[2])

A further point: The true leaders of business transformation rarely reside in the executive suites. Granted, presidents and CEOs can play an important role in removing barriers, providing resources, and giving encouragement, but the spark igniting the change typically comes from the middle—the vice presidents, general managers, program managers, directors, project managers, and functional heads who see an opportunity and begin to run with it. This is one of the great ironies of transformational change: Those who are often seen as lacking the clout, budget, head count, or resources to lead the transformation are often the ones already doing it.

Demonstrate Wisdom, Strength, and Grace

David Spong epitomizes the kind of "antihero," collaborative leader that we consistently encountered in our research. Spong is the president of Aerospace Support (AS) for The Boeing Company. He stands about 5 feet, 7 inches, and is thin, with narrow shoulders. Upon meeting Spong, whose hobby is repairing antique clocks and watches, one could easily mistake him for a British clockmaker. His manner is courteous and polite; his voice soft, with an English accent; his words well chosen, articulate, and thoughtful. In an organization where the majority of senior managers are ex-military officers, many of whom are physically imposing in their appearance and aggressive in their manner, Spong seems almost mouselike by contrast. But if there ever was a mouse that roared, it is David Spong.

Spong downplays nearly all of his accomplishments, attributing the dramatic successes—from playing a key role in the turnaround of the C-17 program, to making AS into one of Boeing's fastest growth businesses—as having more to do with fortunate circumstances and the "magic" of dedicated people than his own leadership. In moments of self-reflection, he even ponders if leadership has more to do with the circumstances you face than the qualities you bring. "Would we even remember who Churchill was today if the Nazis hadn't risen to power?" he asks.

Such comments tell us more about Spong's own self-effacing nature than about how he operates as a leader. This mouse does not wait for circumstances to elevate him; he is an activist in the truest sense of the Henry response. Spong built his entire organization on a foundation of business excellence—it is the strategic imperative for everything he does.

What does business excellence mean to Spong and the people he leads? In its simplest form, it is the seven elements of the Malcolm Baldrige Model (leadership, strategic planning, customers and markets, information and analysis, people focus, process management, and business results) coupled with deep levels of employee involvement and strong organization development practices. Each of these elements helps strengthen the organization to better serve its customers and stakeholders. When applied in a systematic manner (with strong leadership), it is a powerful combination.

Spong's model of leadership is one that we see repeatedly in successful transformational leaders.[3] He exemplifies the discipline of consistently demonstrating wisdom, strength, and grace, even when harried, flustered, and faced with dramatic challenge. See Figure 3.3 for a description of the leadership code.

The image of the all-knowing manager, barking out orders for how to best transform the organization, is laughable to Spong. In his view, power resides in collective learning, having a destination in mind, then solving problems together to jointly build a pathway to the future. Underlying this is a belief in the power of collective wisdom, wisdom that can only be gained through the involvement of others.

The strength Spong demonstrates comes from personal conviction—not physical energy, intimidation, or political clout. Within Boeing, Spong's AS organization is viewed as the living, breathing example of the business excellence philosophy in action. The value of the Baldrige criteria, or the validity of a Baldrige as-

FIGURE 3.3

THE LEADERSHIP CODE

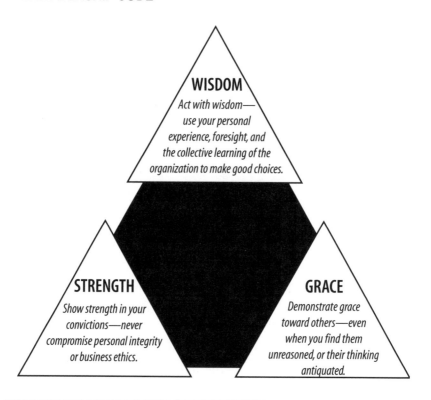

sessment, or the importance of employee involvement, or the role of good organization development practice is not a topic of debate in AS. The focus is on how to improve each element of the model across the entire organization.

Spong's commitment to quality has put him in unprecedented territory—two separate organizations that he has led have won the Malcolm Baldrige Quality Award. Perhaps even more remarkable is that he won the award in two different categories: in 1998 for manufacturing (Airlift and Tanker programs) and in 2003 for service (Aerospace Support). No one else in the history of the award has replicated Spong's remarkable achievement.

Despite his successes, Spong remains a model of grace, which is reflected in his quiet, polite, and introspective nature. In the two organizations Spong has been involved in transforming, he has always given grace to the leaders he has replaced, emphasizing the past accomplishments of his predecessors, rather than focusing on the strategic mistakes or misguided decisions that occurred during their tenure. He does not belittle past decisions in a vain attempt to show how much more effective his program is. Rather, Spong acknowledges the positive aspects of the past, particularly those accomplishments that best reinforce his view of what is needed for the future.

The ability to shape the future of an organization requires people in the organization to be engaged and enthused with leadership—not alienated from it. During moments of adversity and pressure, the manner in which a leader reacts is viewed with the greatest scrutiny. In such moments, if she demonstrates wisdom, strength, and grace, the allegiance of the people in the organization will grow. Acting otherwise, it dissipates.

Reinforce Core, Fundamental Values

Whether or not you are a motorcycle enthusiast, there's a good chance that at some point in your life you've thought about what it would be like to be part of the Harley-Davidson dream: riding across America on a two-wheeled cruiser, the wind in your face, and the feeling of freedom surging through your veins. At the corporate headquarters of the manufacturer of the "world's greatest adult toys," keeping the mystique of the one-hundred-year-old company alive is only part of the challenge. The other part lies in sustaining market dominance against Japanese competitors who have tenfold the engineering, manufacturing, and marketing resources at their disposal.

The company's answer to these challenges is to provide a superior customer experience—in a sense, to help perpetuate the Harley-Davidson dream through the kind of treatment the customer receives from the moment he enters a dealership, to when he is riding down Route 66. No one in the motorcycle industry is more concerned about the entire customer experience—what he sees, how she is treated, the expertise of the service technicians, the responsiveness of the parts counter, the integrity of the finance and insurance (F & I) professional, the friendliness of the sales staff, or the ongoing relationships that are developed through the Harley Owners Group (HOG)—than the Harley-Davidson Motor Company. And the man who is behind the training that Harley-Davidson's 600-plus independently owned dealerships receive is Benny Suggs, director of Harley-Davidson University (HDU).

Suggs is a former U.S. Navy admiral (and a forever motorcycle enthusiast). The only complaint you'll ever hear from him is that he's not getting enough time on the road with his Fat Boy. The rest of what he says is full of raw enthusiasm about the motor company. He talks about where HDU is headed; how great the people are that make up his department; and the wonderful things he sees happening within the dealer network. In fact, Suggs sees all problems as opportunities to further his vision and build a more cohesive team. In his words, "Leadership is best tested in times of adversity."

Upon retiring from the Navy, Suggs was presented with many opportunities in the private sector, but it was Harley-Davidson that got his attention—and not just because of the company's shiny chrome hardware. At Harley-Davidson, Suggs found a consistent set of core values—values that, after three decades of managing officers and sailors, were aligned with what he had come to believe were critical to effective management.

"It was an easy transition to Harley-Davidson because the foundation of values were so consistent with what I believed," notes Suggs. "My job is to reinforce the values every day." The Harley-Davidson values Suggs found so compelling are:

- *Telling the Truth*—Providing full and accurate representation of the facts or situation.
- *Fairness*—Basing decisions and judgments on facts, and carefully considering stakeholders' interests.
- *Keeping Promises*—Doing what you say you're going to do.
- *Respecting the Individual*—Treating all people and institutions with sincerity and dignity.
- *Encouraging Intellectual Curiosity*—Creating an atmosphere that values seeking and applying new knowledge. (See Figure 3.4 for another example of applying core values and principles.)

Within HDU, every tough decision is viewed through the lens of these five values. They serve as a polarizing filter that brings clarity to the many complex decisions that Suggs and the members of his staff face. The values aren't merely encased on the wall in a "Plexiglas tomb" for the curious onlooker to read; they are a part of the day-in, day-out decision making that occurs within the organization. All students of HDU courses learn to recognize the importance of the values, as they appear in virtually every coursebook HDU publishes, and they are referenced by nearly every instructor that speaks.

FIGURE 3.4

THE PRINCIPLES OF MICROSOFT'S STRATEGIC RECRUITING

Harley-Davidson's Benny Suggs wasn't the only leader we interviewed who stressed the importance of values and principles. One of the earliest actions David Pritchard took when he became head of Microsoft's strategic recruiting was to develop a process that led to the creation of a set of core values or principles specific to his organization. The process, which ensured everyone in the organization had the opportunity to provide input, resulted in the *Seven Principles of Strategic Recruiting.*

HIRE QUALITY CANDIDATES
Always uphold the Microsoft recruiting religion. Even in the face of pressures from hiring managers or internal performance measures, recruiting team members must see their role as "the guardians of the threshold." If you have concerns about a candidate, the default is no hire.

OWNERSHIP
Individuals and teams will take on ever-increasing amounts of responsibility and authority.

RESPECT
We treat all candidates, hiring managers, and recruiting team members with dignity and respect.

OPEN AND HONEST COMMUNICATION
Our interactions are open, honest, and direct.

QUALITY AND INNOVATION
We encourage experimentation and risk taking

COMMITMENTS ARE SACRED
We always keep the commitments we make.

HAVE FUN
We see humor, team member relationships, self-expression, and celebration as being critical to our success as an organization.

These principles became so fundamental to the way the organization did business that one would often hear wording taken directly from the document and used in everyday conversation among the recruiters. Phrases like "Uphold the religion"; "That commitment is sacred"; Let's celebrate these results" became common expressions within the department. This is a key point—to create a principle-based organization, the principles must be used and applied in a regular and consistent manner. The value is in the consistent application of the principles to help address issues or exploit opportunities. Ideally, the principles become so widely understood and applied that they become part of the organization's vernacular.

To the cynical, phrases like "Tell the truth," "Be fair," and "Keep your promises" might sound more like Boy Scout mottoes, or words of wisdom from kindergarten teachers, than the foundation on which to run a multibillion-dollar corporation. Yet, in a post-Enron/Tyco/WorldCom era, these simple values resonate. As Arthur Andersen learned, the damage of a single betrayal, or a single breach of trust, cannot be overestimated. By colluding with its Enron clients, shredding documents to help cover up accounting abuses, the company that once set the standard for accounting excellence was destroyed. Where were the signposts to redirect the behavior? Where was the obsession with values when it really mattered?

By demonstrating adherence to its values, Harley-Davidson has become one of the most respected companies in the United States. In the most recent Harris Interactive ranking of the best and worst reputations among American corporations, the Harley-Davidson Motor Company ranked second. Not surprisingly, Enron ranked dead last of the sixty companies evaluated, followed closely by its partner in crime, Andersen Worldwide (number fifty-seven on the list).[4]

Successful leaders have a foundation of values that are regularly referenced and applied in a consistent manner, becoming a tool to help guide behavior. This pattern is no accident: The consistent application of core values creates committed followers. In fact, the difference in bottom-line performance between managers who followers view as acting with integrity versus managers who are seen as unscrupulous is significant. A recent study showed that the single feature having the greatest impact on profitability performance (when comparing organizations of similar size, complexity, and market opportunity) was the degree of integrity employees saw in the organization's leadership.[5] In other words, acting with integrity is not just good from an ethical sense, it is also a means of increased employee trust and organization profit.

This same story has been played out at HDU under Benny Suggs's value-driven leadership. In the last two years, the university has increased the number of students it serves by 69 percent, while maintaining one of the highest customer satisfaction ratings in the company. During that same period, the organization's budget has dropped by $1 million. It has received several awards, including recognition as the world's best corporate university for technical training and the 2003 winner of the prestigious Corporate University Xchange Award for e-learning. The bottom line: more service, less cost, and better results.

Empower Others—Across All Levels in the Organization—To Take Action

When David Pritchard became the head of Microsoft's strategic recruiting, he inherited an organization that had just been through what one consultant at the time described as "the worst reorganization I've ever seen." Even though Pritchard had nothing to do with developing the new organization structure (an ambitious, if misguided, attempt to gain greater economy of scale by combining campus and experienced hire recruiting), the fact that he had been selected to lead it by those who were behind it created a strong "guilt by association."

The situation was so bad that over half of the remaining employees in the department had verbally stated that they were planning to leave as soon as other employment opportunities within the company emerged. When reviewing the data, Pritchard himself become so distraught that, just a few weeks into the position, he seriously wondered if he could ever be successful in managing the strategic recruiting organization. Trust was low, talented people were ready to leave in droves, and the pressure to increase the number of hires in order to feed the company's insatiable appetite for software engineers was about to double.

Pritchard responded by emphasizing a high-involvement leadership style, actively gaining the trust of his staff by soliciting their views on how to turn the organization around. He began weekly team meetings, inviting everyone in the department to attend, where he'd review the organization's performance, then seek feedback on how to improve it. This was soon followed by the formation of project teams that were empowered to streamline processes and implement new systems. To perpetuate the high-involvement work culture, Pritchard attempted to keep the organization as flat as possible, at one point having fifty direct reports.

The accomplishments Pritchard oversaw were stunning—in his nearly nine-year tenure (1994 to 2002) as the head of recruiting, over 17,000 people were hired, most of whom were key contributors to such breakthrough products as Windows 98, Office 97, Office 98 for Macintosh, Windows 2000, Windows XP, and MSN. He was featured in *Fortune* magazine as the man who had helped create the recruiting machine that kept Microsoft the world's preeminent company in its ability to "attract, develop, and retain top talent." Despite the planning sessions he oversaw, the countless meetings he held, the ongoing training he approved, and the refining of processes and systems that occurred, Pritchard maintains a remarkably simple view on how the success of the recruiting organization was achieved. In his words, "A leader listens to his or her people, sets the boundaries, and then lets them run with it. If you are successful, you soon learn that it's not about 'your vision' because the ultimate goal is for the people you manage to feel ownership for the future success of the organization. So, in reality, it's all about 'their vision.'"

The future shaper recognizes that change requires the dedication and commitment of the people in the organization. Leadership is not a "Lone Ranger" act; it is a people-intensive vocation that begins with providing direction, setting boundaries, and then empowering others.

Dedicate Tremendous Time and Energy to "Overcommunicating" the Future

The point David Pritchard makes is a good one to remember when attempting to set the "vision" for an organization: It's not about what the leader thinks; it's about what the people in the organization think. The idea isn't to create a view of the future that only resides in the heads of a few executives. It's to create a picture that everyone can understand, recognize, and help implement.

If you want to find out what the *real* vision is in an organization, listen in on the lunchtime conversations of employees, or check out what people are saying about the company in a corporate chat room. The topics that dominate their conversation, how they describe where the organization is headed, what they see as its priorities for the future—this is the "real" vision of tomorrow. More often than not, the view of the future held by the employees is at odds with the view of the leadership team.

Harvard professor, business consultant, and author John Kotter is fond of pointing out that managers typically undercommunicate large-scale change efforts by a factor of at least ten to one hundred times.[6] In the book *Competing for the Future,* authors Gary Hamel and C.K. Prahalad come to a similar conclusion, pointing out that the average senior management team only spends about 2.4 percent of its time developing a collective view of how the organization needs to operate in the future.[7] Simply put, undercommunication is chronic.

Why is undercommunication so pervasive? For one thing, communication is typically an afterthought. After hours and days spent thinking through a critical decision, only a few minutes are typically dedicated to how the decision will be communicated. This lack of planning and preparation shows. When the message is delivered, it often lacks timeliness and appears confused, and it is often delivered by the wrong person.

A second problem with communication is the belief that "flowing down" a message is an effective way to communicate it across a large organization. A typical flow-down begins when each department head takes the message from her boss, then retells it to her managers. Those managers then flow it down to the next level, which, in turn, flows it down to the next and so on, until the entire organization eventually hears the message. The reality of this communication approach is that after the second or third translation, the message has already become confused. In fact, it is not unlike the game of telephone that children play in elementary school. Further, as the communication moves deeper and deeper into the organization, the person who is responsible for doing the communicating is farther and farther removed from the rationale that led to it in the first place.

Recognizing this common communication shortfall, many executives hold assemblies so that they have the opportunity to speak directly to everyone in their organization. We observed how effectively Fred Hanson did this during the astonishing turnaround in the Tektronix portables division in the 1980s, and how well Boeing's Vice President of Naval Aircraft Programs, Pat Finneran, uses assemblies to keep the execution of the change on target today. Quaker Oats Director Steve Brunner, who also used regular assemblies during his tenure as the plant manager at the company's Danville, Illinois, operation, believed that some messages were best delivered not by telling people, but by showing them.

Shortly after the ratification of the North American Free Trade Act (NAFTA), Brunner recognized that the door had been opened for companies like Quaker to relocate plants to Mexico in search of cheaper labor and lower production costs. In fact, the only way for a U.S.–based plant to compete would be by demonstrating dramatically better productivity and quality performance that kept its cost per case at, or below, what could be done in Mexico. Brunner also knew that the current performance at the Danville plant didn't cut it. Without some significant improvements, it would price itself out of business.

Communicating the case for change wasn't getting Brunner very far—particularly among union members, who were skeptical about his real intentions. Was there really a cost gap, or was Brunner merely attempting to gain concessions from them? So, rather than continuing to tell the union leadership the case for change, Brunner decided to show them. He and seven others from the Danville plant (four managers and four union members) toured five different manufacturing plants in Juarez and Mexico City.

Everyone was stunned by the efficiency and lack of waste in the operations, as well as the professionalism and enthusiasm of the workforce. By *showing the message,* Brunner gained the support of union leader John Pigg, who would play a pivotal role in the turnaround of the Danville operation. This event marked the beginning of a union/management partnership that led *Industry Week* magazine to select Quaker's Danville, Illinois, facility as a recipient of their prestigious "Ten Best Plants in America Award" in 1998.

"Overcommunicating" the future is not the same as "overselling" it. When we speak of communicating the change, we mean creating a means where an ongoing dialogue can occur. Leadership and employees alike provide information, insight, and feedback to the organization direction. People across the organization are engaged because they have a common knowledge, and they have been part of ongoing dialogues about where the organization is headed.

Selling the change often requires that promises are made. Often the communication is not in the form of dialogue, but in a one-way format. The leader tries to sell the employee an idea, and he delivers the message with little or no feedback from the person receiving it. In our experience, if large amounts of time are being spent "selling" the change, the effort may be in trouble.

Seek Short-Term Successes

Transformational change rarely happens quickly. By definition, it is a long-term effort. How long? It would be unusual for a major transformation of a large, complex organization to take less than three to seven years. Given this fact, most experts emphasize the importance of keeping a long-term perspective and not anticipating immediate results. This is a logical argument from a rational viewpoint. The pressures that exist in organizations—and the forces against change in particular—are not, however, rational. Based on our experience, if some significant milestone cannot be achieved quickly (within the first three months to one year), the change effort may not receive the support it needs to ever succeed over the long haul.

As with many aspects of leadership, the future shaper must recognize this contradiction. On the one hand, for the change to be fully implemented and a new organization culture to truly emerge, years of effort will be required. Yet, if significant improvement is not achieved within months, the budget and resources to see the change through will never materialize. This is the yin and yang of shaping the future: Stay focused on the long term, while ensuring continuous short-term successes.

The bottom line is that highly visible, achievable, and short-term goals need to be planned into the effort. The transition plan should be filled with opportunities to demonstrate early success, and it should clearly show forward progress. And once the success is achieved, it must be given lots of visibility so that it becomes widely recognized across the entire organization. Immediate success helps keep those with the budget and resources engaged in the effort, and it has the secondary benefit of lessening resistance to the change. As one general manager noted, "There's nothing like a little success to keep the skeptics at bay."

The leadership team at one food company consciously adopted this approach. Recognizing the need to cut production costs, they first set what they felt was a readily achievable target of $3 million in cost savings. Once the goal was achieved, they celebrated it as a significant milestone, and then provided additional resources for employee training, including how to work on teams and how to use specific problem-solving methods. The next milestone—an additional $4 million in cost savings—was soon achieved. Again, a celebration and additional resources added to the effort. As one manager noted, "We go as far as we can see, and then we take a look at the next horizon." As each improvement milestone is achieved, it is celebrated, further strengthening the resolve and commitment to the effort. Leadership now believes cost savings of $25 million are doable.

Leverage Serendipity to Influence Direction

For those who have never seen "mahogany row," it may come as a surprise that the most effective executives tend to utilize "informal" channels to gain support for their plans, rather than relying solely on structured meetings and formal communiqués that flow down through the hierarchy. While much important work gets done through the formal channels of the weekly staff meetings, two-day off-sites, planning sessions, and program reviews, this is only half the story. The chance encounter in the parking lot with a key team member, the five-minute chat with a peer on the way to lunch, and an impromptu thirty-minute gathering of key staff members are often even more important in getting decisions made and creating change in the organization.

The future shaper recognizes this organizational reality: Many critical decisions are influenced, and often decided, long before they ever appear on the agenda of the weekly staff meeting. The key is gaining access to the right people, getting the chance to present the case, and then encouraging them to support it. This is the informal realm of influencing and decision making.

Unlike formal organizational linkages, influencing through informal channels often appears random, chaotic, and by happenstance. Yet, for the effective leader, informal channels leave far less to "dumb luck" and chance than might initially appear. In fact, managers who are particularly adept at influencing change are able to *leverage serendipity* with seeming ease. They, in fact, create "chance" encounters that enable them to gain access to the individuals whose support they desperately need.

How can one truly leverage serendipity and use it to influence corporate direction? It begins by carefully identifying who it is that needs to be influenced in order to move the transformation effort forward. Once the *target* is identified, the best *means of influence* is determined. Finally, the future shaper begins *opportunity scripting,* literally planning ways to gain the required face time to get her position heard.

This influencing dance plays itself out in many ways. A Corning manager adopted the exact same schedule as his target—an executive two levels above her in the management hierarchy. Every day, by arriving and leaving work at the same time, the odds of a "chance" encounter with her target increased. Over the course of several months, the manager had dozens of five-minute conversations that would have otherwise never occurred. As a result of her "chance" encounters, she was able to influence an important corporate project.

Another future shaper used an office move as an opportunity to get his desk as physically close to his target—a division vice president—as he could. He explained, "By getting my desk here I'm guaranteed a short conversation nearly every day. That's a lot of influencing opportunities!"

While such strategies might seem contrived, it remains true that positions on many key organizational issues are developed outside formal meetings and strategy sessions. By being an activist and seeking to leverage serendipity, the future shaper increases the likelihood that his position will be, at the very least, heard and, at the very best, adopted.

The case for being effective at leveraging serendipity is also strengthened when one views those who are not good at it. Those who consistently surprise their boss in formal settings (with strategies or tactics that have not been previously discussed) are the most common example. In one instance with which we are familiar, the chief executive officer of a Fortune 500 company was completely caught off guard when the president of one of the company's divisions made a recommendation to close down a production line. The recommendation was so far removed from what the CEO and other members of the executive team were expecting that the idea was quickly shot down. While the merits of what he was proposing were actually quite good, the president had completely failed to prepare his audience for the "surprise" in the days and weeks prior to the meeting. Thus, his failure was inevitable. The president failed to influence the outcome and, consequently, did not obtain the result he had hoped for.

The point is simple: Every conversation is a chance to move an idea. Create opportunities to have lots of conversations with those whose support is critical to the success of the change. Waiting an hour for a two-minute "chance" encounter could be the best use of your time.

Execute with Tenacity

In 1994, the head of the health-care unit of a major U.S. insurance carrier unveiled a daring vision—the decentralization of the company's health-care practice, moving from the one centralized group it currently had to ten regional offices. Each regional office would have the responsibility and authority to address the unique requirements of that region, from signing contracts with health-care providers, to developing plans that would be attractive to customers in that region, to setting regional cost targets. Those in the field, long frustrated by the centralized command and control structure, applauded the vision.

In just over two years, the whole effort was abandoned. No more than two regional offices were ever put in place, and both were shut down just over a year after their opening. The visionary who initiated the effort was demoted and replaced by a man who had been the harshest critic of his plan. The company slowly cut back on their health-care offerings, as they found it increasingly difficult to compete in various regions of the country. Today, the firm doesn't offer any health-care coverage at all. What happened?

While there were many factors that contributed to this outcome (such as the resistance of central office employees who didn't want to relocate), the effort ultimately failed because of the plan's execution. In a nutshell, the strategy was sound, the plan was solid, but the execution was dismal.

Compare this fiasco to the approach the insurance giant CIGNA is taking as it strives to transform itself into a "customer-oriented enterprise." A key change in achieving this goal was to move away from a line of business structure to a process-oriented one, requiring the adoption of common processes across the entire company. By using a common set of processes across CIGNA, a whole new level of service became possible to not only better meet the needs of discrete markets, but of individual customers as well. Today clients can, for example, log onto "myCIGNA.com" and get complete information on not only their health-care plan, but also the status of their retirement accounts. This approach gives customers an unprecedented amount of control over their individual benefit needs. It has taken years to develop and, at different points, met considerable resistance, but leadership saw the execution through.[8]

This brings us to our seventh, and critically important, leadership discipline—the ability to execute plans. So much has been written about the need for leaders to establish vision and to focus their thinking on the future that it seems to imply their role should be almost esoteric, removed from the day-in, day-out issues that abound in organizations. In reality, leaders must give attention to detail, be clear about accountability, and ensure follow-through on actions. They must be good at doing the hard, repetitive, and often tedious work of ensuring that their plans are executed.

Leaders who are good at execution—like Boeing's Pat Finneran—are very predictable. They systematically review performance, employ a means to grade its progress, and quickly spot and address trends of underachievement that might impact the ability of the plan to succeed. Expectations and accountabilities are crystal clear.

Without the discipline of execution, everything else—the great strategy, the brilliant vision, the beautiful goal, and the energized workforce—means nothing.

A Final Thought

A discipline, when applied consistently, becomes a habitual, unconscious act. The most effective leaders are those who live and breathe the transformation that they advocate. The message is consistent, the direction clear, the effort untiring. It is as if the change exudes from their very pores. The seven disciplines of leadership outlined here form a critical foundation for those aspiring to lead their organization into the future.

The leader who seeks to shape the future will encounter many obstacles along the way, including resisters. There will be those who outwardly resist the change, and those who use political connections to derail the effort through subtle means. It is with some irony, though, that the greatest obstacle of all will be the limitations and fears of the leader and the team he leads. For the leader, transforming an organization is not just about changing others; it is also about accepting change within oneself.

While a foundation of strong leadership is critical in transforming complex organizations, by itself it is not enough. Transformation requires a systematic approach—a pathway that aligns the people, systems, and processes within the organization to the transformation cause. And it all begins with defining the future.

Notes

1. Rhonda Britten notes that our fears tend to keep us in certain patterns of behavior, what she refers to as the "wheel of fear." The

alternative way to behave is to make choices, not from a sense of fear, but from a sense of freedom. Only when we are operating from the "wheel of freedom," Britten contends, can we enjoy fearless living. See Rhonda Britten, *Fearless Living: Live Without Excuses and Love Without Regret* (New York: Perigee, 2001).

2. Rakesh Khurana, "The Curse of the Superstar CEO," *Harvard Business Review,* September 2002.

3. In many ways David Spong epitomizes what Jim Collins refers to as "level five" leadership in his book *Good to Great.* Collins's observations that the most effective leaders are those who develop their leadership team and speak of what others have accomplished, often downplaying their own achievements, are exactly what we experienced during our interviews with David Spong. For more insight into "level five" leadership, see Jim Collins, *Good to Great* (New York: HarperCollins, 2001).

4. Ronald Alsop, "Scandal-Filled Year Takes Toll on Companies' Good Names," *The Wall Street Journal,* February 12, 2003.

5. Tim Simons, "The High Cost of Trust," in the forethought section of the *Harvard Business Review*, September 2002.

6. John Kotter, *Leading Change* (Boston, Mass.: Harvard Business School Press, 1996).

7. Gary Hamel and C.K. Prahalad, *Competing for the Future* (Boston, Mass.: Harvard Business School Press, 1994), p. 4.

8. Anthony O'Donnell, "Paradigm Shift," *Insurance & Technology,* October 2002, pp. 29–30.

THE SIMPLE VIEW:
Establishing the Bridge to the Future

In the early 1990s, a senior manager of a division of a major defense contractor formed a task force to try and understand why the organization's rate of performance improvement was so dismally low. The task force began its work by interviewing a cross section of managers in an effort to gain a clearer picture of what was happening on a day-to-day basis within the division. The findings were surprising. Issues such as compliance to government contract stipulations, or inadequate technology, or poor skill development didn't make the list. Rather, the task force learned that managers were responsible for twenty-seven change initiatives, yet no one single manager (including the executives within the division) could name more than four of these initiatives. Further, how the initiatives were linked (and who was accountable for them) had never been presented, or even fully discussed within management ranks. The task force concluded that a lack of clear direction and priorities was crippling performance.

While this lack of focus seemed incredible to us at the time, we've since learned that this organization was, by no means, unique. In a more recent example, we discovered a division of a U.S. automotive manufacturer that had 235 separate initiatives going on at once! Imagine being a manager in such an organization, responsible for ensuring that progress for the year is being made against 200 discrete initiatives. Assuming you know each initiative inside and out, that gives you approximately one business day to work on each initiative—assuming, of course, that you have no other responsibilities competing for your time. It seems preposterous to even consider implementing two or three significant changes at once, but 235? Predictably, this organization is filled with cynicism about the programs that management seems to introduce at its whim.

This tendency to layer on program after program to address an emerging problem or a new opportunity, without careful consideration for how it fits into the vision and overall direction of the organization, is all too common. The result? Organizations expend tremendous energy in a variety of different, often competing directions. With energy so wildly dispersed among varied (and even contradictory) priorities, change cannot be sustained. It lacks clear focus, direction, logic, and alignment. Further, it is an utterly reactive approach, with little thought given to what is needed for future success. Finally, it hurts management's credibility with the very employees who will ultimately be responsible for implementing the change. It lessens the possibility of achieving transformational change across the organization due to the vast dilution of energy and focus.

Fog of Bureaucracy

"The fog of war" is the point in a battle when information channels break down and confusion reigns across the field. While engulfed in this cloud of miscommunication, decisions are sometimes made that needlessly endanger lives and, in the extreme, lead an army to shoot—and ultimately kill—its own men. While engulfed in the fog of war, an army can literally destroy itself, while its enemy idly watches.[1]

Many organizations today are engulfed in a similar fog of misinformation and confusion—a state we refer to as the *fog of bureaucracy* (see Figure 4.1 for a description of the characteristics of "bureaucratic fog"). It is an outgrowth of steep management hierarchies, narrowly defined work roles, complex matrix structures, rigid departmental boundaries, and countless "high-priority" initiatives that serve to distort attention and focus. The average employee finds himself in a shroud of dense confusion about direction and priorities. And, in this confusion, the employee works diligently on what are often the wrong objectives. The organization begins destroying its competitive position from the inside.

How is the fog of bureaucracy perpetuated? It is a result of classic thinking about organization structure, hierarchy, and the role of specialization—thinking that was developed during the early 1900s, long before the explosion of information technology, the profound advances in the social sciences, and the emergence of global competition. While they are outdated, classic bureaucratic approaches remain pervasive, and, to many, it is difficult (if not impossible) to imagine organizations operating any other way.

Bureaucratic fog creates inherent resistance to change: Normal information channels are largely ineffective; it is in the best interest of those in power to perpetuate the status quo; integrating the various departments, functions, and programs in a unified direction is exceedingly difficult. The result is that, at every opportunity to initiate change, there are well-established counterforces acting against it.

The contrast between classic and modern views of the practice

FIGURE 4.1

PERPETUATING THE FOG

The characteristics of the bureaucratic fog include:

POLICY WORSHIP

In order to maintain a sense of fairness and equity across a large organization, there is a natural tendency to rely on an extensive framework of policies and rules that are often contradictory and reinforce behaviors that have a negative effect on the organization.

COMPLEXITY ACCEPTANCE

Given the choice between simple or complex approaches, the complex approach usually wins out. Underlying this tendency is the view that the organization is inherently complex so it needs sophisticated solutions to address the problems it faces.

ASSUMPTION OF ELSEWHERE

Due to its complexity, no one has a complete picture of the workings of the entire organization. Often, the assumption is made that people in other departments are dealing with issues or business opportunities that, in fact, are not being addressed by anyone at all.

AVERSION TO INTEGRATION

When Max Weber first conceptualized the notion of bureaucracy, he wanted to create a structure where departments with narrowly defined specialties dealt with issues on an impersonal, unbiased basis. Bureaucracy is inherently focused on specialization—integrating separate groups, functions, or departments and getting them to work toward a common goals takes significant energy and effort.

PROTECTION OF FIEFDOMS

One's power base is related to the pressures (either positive or negative) that her department can exert on other organizations. There is a tendency for managers to seek to expand the influence of their function, department, or group, even if it is not necessarily in the best interest of the company, in order to strengthen their power base.

of management is profound (see Figure 4.2). Having a well-defined hierarchy that follows a strict chain of command is a fundamental feature in the old view, but it becomes nearly meaningless in organizations designed around accessing and applying knowledge—the modern view. Where specialization was paramount in yesterday's thinking, integrating specialized abilities to more quickly bring solutions to customers is the hallmark of the new order. Whereas ensuring employee compliance was seen as a key part of the manager's role in the past, gaining employee commitment is seen as the foundation of leadership for the future.

We often observe fierce arguments in which bright, articulate managers declare, "Our structure must match the inherent complexity that resides within our organization." The result is often the

FIGURE 4.2

CLASSIC VS. MODERN MANAGEMENT

CLASSIC MANAGEMENT	MODERN MANAGEMENT
• Hierarchy-driven	• Knowledge-driven
• Specialization	• Integration of specialties
• Complexity	• Simplicity
• Protect	• Expand
• Compliance-oriented	• Commitment-oriented
• Multiple initiatives	• Integrated plan

creation of complex matrix structures—sometimes needing three-dimensional drawings to describe the relationship between functions, programs, geography, shifts, initiatives, councils, projects, offices . . . you name it. While the complexity is cleverly depicted in graphic form, a fundamental question is often ignored: How will the work actually get accomplished under the structure? And, as one looks at the complex structure, the obscure reporting relationships, the unclear roles, it's easy to recognize that work will get done, but *is it because of the structure, or in spite of it?*

Complexity breeds greater complexity. Multiple organizations vie for limited budget, head count, information, and recognition by establishing their own set of initiatives that are deemed fundamental to meeting the unique needs of the stakeholders they serve. Left unchecked, the initiatives propagate into the tens—even hundreds—as each function or program seeks to gain the maximum amount of management time, energy, and attention. Often, the sheer volume of initiatives becomes so great that it dilutes management focus and energy, ensuring that little change actually gets implemented.

The Problem with Vision

A clear vision of the future helps create a greater sense of alignment, and it *should* help to more greatly focus initiatives. But, in reality, the word "vision" has become an almost useless term for describing leadership's role in setting direction. Its meaning within organizations ranges from platitudes—"We will uphold the highest ethical standards in our industry"—to specific financial targets— "We will grow revenue by 5 percent next year." In fact, if you were to graph the types of so-called vision statements that leaders articulate, you would see a tendency toward these two extremes—

either a grandiose statement, or a very specific metric. Such visions actually increase confusion about future direction, rather than clarify the situation.

In studying why CEOs and company presidents drive so little large-scale change in organizations (as we said earlier, the notion that change must be driven by the highest-level executive is a myth; most large-scale transformations are actually driven by managers several layers below the president's office), Harvard's Michael Beer (along with Russell Eisenstat and Bert Spector) observed that executives are so far removed from the "real" work, that they tend to talk about change in grand statements and platitudes.[2] Their statements are typically so broad that any program or initiative that a midlevel manager might develop can be rationalized as fitting into the future "vision."

The other extreme, the narrowly defined metric, tends to perpetuate a reactive, short-term view within the management ranks, and it often results in cynicism about the future. What people see are incremental improvements to meet a new demand, not a forward look at what the organization could become in the future. The sense across the organization is that "we're squeezing the turnip again" to get the next percentage point or two of quality improvement, cost savings, or revenue increase (or whatever the goal is). The broader view of what the organization could become, what its future looks like, and how these incremental improvements help achieve this greater purpose are never described.

A Detailed View of the Future

Neither of these perspectives is useful in aligning effort within the organization. Further, each approach degrades the use of vision as a tool for achieving focus and alignment within the organization. Our definition of vision attempts to find the middle ground between these two extremes (see Figure 4.3). In our view a vision is: A detailed description of a desired future that provides clarity as to how the organization will need to operate differently in order to meet the changing conditions of its markets, customers, and overall business environment.

FIGURE 4.3

DEVELOPING A MEANINGFUL VISION

ABSTRACT	DESCRIPTION OF THE POSSIBLE FUTURE	SPECIFIC
• Platitudes • Grandiose statements *Broad and grandiose statements that provide too little detail about the future.*	• A vivid description of the future *Describes a possible future in enough detail to engage people— they are able to see what could be possible.*	• Short-term goals and metrics • Financial targets *Short-term, metric-focused goals that perpetuate incremental improvement.*

Our approach to vision development results in the creation of a *strategic visualization of the future*. For Pat Finneran, the vice president and general manager of Boeing's Naval Aircraft Programs, the need to paint a picture of the future for his organization became very clear in October 2001, when Boeing learned that it had lost the Joint Strike Fighter (JSF) program—the single largest defense contract ever awarded and potentially worth $200 billion to $400 billion—to its archrival, Lockheed Martin.[3] Finneran had not been involved with the JSF project team, but he well imagined the frustration its members felt. In the aftermath of the loss, the very future of the St. Louis site was filled with uncertainty.

Unlike major defense contracts of the past, the JSF was truly a winner-take-all, multibillion-dollar bonanza. Finishing second guaranteed Boeing nothing, not even a minor subcontracting role. The development and manufacture of the next generation of warfighter, a single aircraft that was intended to meet the needs of the Air Force, Army, Navy, and Marines for decades to come, was in sole possession of Lockheed Martin.

As Pat Finneran looked across his organization in the aftershock of the loss, he saw a product line that, without changes, was destined for obsolescence when the JSF reached full production less than a decade into the future. While the short-term outlook of naval aircraft programs was good—under Finneran's leadership significant operational gains had been made in efficiency, cost, and quality, which contributed to its impressive financial performance—its future viability looked bleak.

At a fundamental level, Finneran, and many others among his leadership team, recognized that the value proposition of Naval Aircraft Programs had to change. In the past, the organization had focused on improving its operational effectiveness, and the results were impressive. The future, however, required a focus on innovation and closer customer contact (what become known as increased "customer intimacy"). While at a strategic level, greater innovation and customer intimacy made intellectual sense, Finneran still faced the challenge of translating this abstract idea into a clear picture of how he and the members of his team would operate differently on a day-to-day basis.

It is at this point—the point of translating a vision into practical application—where many executives fail. They see what needs to be done at a high level, but they are unable to describe it in a meaningful way to those whose support is most critical to its success. This was part of Finneran's effectiveness: the art of translation.

Finneran, a Notre Dame graduate and former Marine Corps flight officer, knew the importance of developing a crystal-clear picture of the future, and then following a disciplined process for sustaining progress toward it. So, one of his early actions was to oversee the creation of a vivid description of the future. It was to be a description that showed how Naval Aircraft Programs would operate as a truly innovative, customer-intimate organization.

The Mechanics of Vision

The document that was created described such things as the use of cross-functional "solution teams" to address new opportunities; a customer-relationship management system, enabling seamless customer contact; a more diverse workforce, including top university graduates; a two-time improvement in development; and a change in how Finneran's staff would spend their time. (They would now have a more balanced focus that would include operations, customer intimacy, and solutions leadership, instead of one that concentrated exclusively on operational issues.) Consider this passage from the document:

> To achieve the goal of keeping the F/A-18 competitive in the future with the JSF (F-35) and tough European competitors, the Naval Aircraft Programs leadership team recognized that it needed to shift the value proposition of the organization. This shift has created a better balance

between operational excellence, customer intimacy, and solutions leadership.

Operational excellence, long the hallmark of the organization, has continued to lead to the continuous improvement in cost, schedule, and time to market. A greater focus on customer intimacy has led to a much broader influence in procurement decisions. Further, the perception of the F/A-18 aircraft as a legacy system has changed. It is now seen as critical to the Department of Defense vision of network-centric battle space. The F/A-18, with its relatively low cost and superior knowledge management systems, which serves to multiple combat effectiveness, has demonstrated how the Naval Aircraft Programs organization has broadened its capabilities from providing superior products to demonstrating true solutions leadership.

Members of the Naval Aircraft Programs leadership team spend the majority of their time addressing strategic, future-oriented issues. Today, nearly 60 percent to 70 percent of the time of members of the leadership team is spent in the areas of customer development and business growth (managing external relations); long-term planning, strategy, and communication across the organization (managing direction); mentoring and developing individuals and teams (developing people); creating a culture where innovation and change are encouraged

(managing innovation and change); and the coordination of program and functional activities across Naval Aircraft Programs, ensuring alignment and integration
(managing coordination). Less than 30 percent to 40 percent of leadership time is spent in addressing day-to-day
operational issues. The current profile of how members
of the Naval Aircraft Programs leadership team spend
their time is in sharp contrast to how it was just five years
ago, when the majority of time was spent dealing with
operational issues and reacting to customer requests
(see Figure 4.4).

The shift to becoming more strategic, growth, and long-
term focused was enabled by a solid, systematic approach to delegating many tasks formerly done at the
vice president and director level to those lower in the organization. Improvements to systems, processes, training, and a strong commitment to employee involvement
have helped move decision making lower in the organization and further improve operations. The shift was purposeful and began when Naval Aircraft Programs took a
serious look at the value proposition of "solutions leadership" and "customer intimacy" as the key to future
growth. Over time, the leadership team recognized that
greater customer intimacy required more focus on cus-
tomer-related issues—customer relationship building, increasing influence with key think tanks and influencers,
shifting from "platform-centric" to "solution-centric," and
developing the capability to provide a comprehensive
"solutions package" to customers.

FIGURE 4.4

SHIFTING HOW LEADERSHIP SPENDS ITS TIME

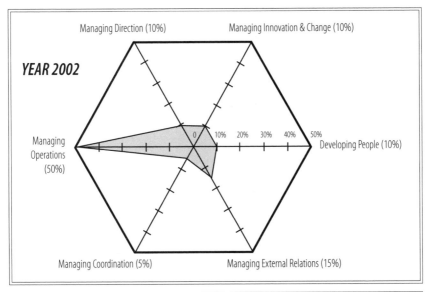

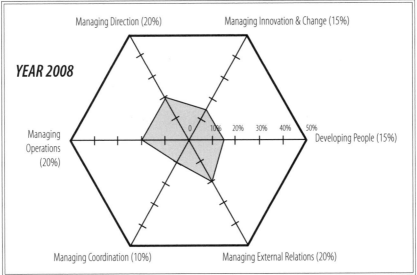

The idea of using a spider diagram to depict how managers utilize their time was first introduced to us by Geoff Peppiatt, founder of the U.K. consulting firm Pratick, Ltd. Peppiatt recognized the extraordinary power that creating a visual representation of how managers spend their time could have in getting them to think about how to shift their priorities.

A typical agenda of the leadership team reflects the emphasis on solutions leadership, customer intimacy, and longer-range planning.

Leadership Team Agenda: 2008

1. Focus on people
2. Business results
3. Market assessment report-outs
4. Customer feedback and opportunities
5. International opportunities assessment
6. Market share and competition report
7. Solutions teams report-out
8. Long-term strategy milestone review
9. Spanning solutions briefing
10. Business excellence review

Notice how the description is written as an *affirmation*, as if the events it is describing have already occurred. The author initially wrote the piece as if he were looking backward from now, writing in the year 2008 about how the organization had changed. This style of writing serves three important purposes: (1) it excites the imagination by describing what could be; (2) it is written as if it has already occurred, creating a sense that the described future is truly possible; and (3) it provides enough detail to give a clear sense of how behaviors, roles, processes, and priorities will need to be different in the future (see Figure 4.5).

In our experience, many managers simply lack either the imagination to develop a detailed description of the future, or the

FIGURE 4.5
_____

THE DEFINITION OF A DETAILED DESCRIPTION

> A detailed description of the organization in a strategically significant position at a point in the future. The future is described as if it has already occurred, enabling people to visualize how the organization will operate when the future point is achieved.

courage to actually articulate it. The most powerful visions we have seen for gaining alignment require both these traits—imagination and courage. Furthermore, they go beyond describing the general direction the organization is headed: They utilize the vision to firmly state its destination (see Figure 4.6).

Boiling It All Down—The Strategic Imperative

The intent of the vivid description is to provide a glimpse into what the future could be, written in enough detail to describe how roles, processes, and systems will be changed in order to improve the organization's competitive position. It provides a perspective beyond what direction the organization is headed; it actually describes what the organization will look like when its future arrives.

While this detailed view of the future provides a picture of the destination, it does not provide the means to achieve it. And, while we have clarity as to what we are after, the potential for energy to become dispersed among different priorities remains high. As we have emphasized in previous chapters, knowing the destination is important, but getting an entire organization moving along the

(text continues on page 126)

FIGURE 4.6

THE MECHANICS OF CREATING A DETAILED DESCRIPTION OF A POSSIBLE FUTURE

There is considerable research to indicate what we've intuitively known for years—companies with a clear vision of their future consistently outperform companies where the sense of direction is clouded and unclear.[*] In fact, a concrete vision about the future is a critical trait in assuring long-term organizational success. Companies, organizations, teams, individuals ultimately move toward—and often become—the future they have envisioned.

If the leadership of an organization has not clearly described a possible future, a vision by default will emerge. The default vision assumes existing processes, practices, and skills are adequate for the organization to prosper—that the future will essentially be a continuation of the past. If leadership does not clearly define and gain widespread commitment to a future vision, the result is the continuation of what is already known and practiced—the status quo.

To create a vivid description of a possible future, the following process has proven to be highly effective:

1. THE LEADERSHIP TEAM DETERMINES THE APPROPRIATE TIME HORIZON FOR THE VISION.
The vision for a large corporation should probably span a decade or more. The vision for a division might span 5-10 years. A plant might look out 5 years. For a team, a 2- year time frame might be more appropriate. As a general guideline, the larger the organization, the further out the vision of the future should be.

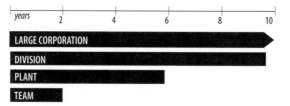

2. A COMPREHENSIVE ENVIRONMENTAL SCAN OF THE THREATS AND OPPORTUNITIES THAT ORGANIZATION IS LIKELY TO FACE IS DEVELOPED.

Scenario planning is one tool that is enormously effective in getting a grasp on the likely environmental conditions the organization will face. This process begins by looking at the best-case, worst-case developments and their potential impact on the business over a specific time horizon.

3. DEVELOP INTERVIEW QUESTIONS BASED AROUND AN ORGANIZATIONAL MODEL.

There are countless models that can be used to organize the questions and the manner in which the data is reviewed. In the case of Naval Aircraft Programs, the model utilized was business excellence. It examines the areas of: leadership; strategic planning; customer and market focus; information and analysis; people focus; process management; and business results. The questions should be open ended and built around the time frame defined in step one.

4. INTERVIEW THE LEADERSHIP TEAM OF THE ORGANIZATION, ASKING THEM TO DESCRIBE THEIR VISION OF THE FUTURE.

Envisioning a positive future is—in our experience—more difficult for people than citing the various problems they currently face. Secondly, when describing the future, people often tend to describe it in vague and generic terms. Attempt to combat both of these tendencies by asking questions that require detailed responses. To further help frame their responses, ask interviewees to describe a future they believe has at least a 50-50 chance of happening.

5. DEVELOP AN INITIAL DRAFT OF THE DESCRIPTION OF THE FUTURE BASED ON THE DATA GAINED DURING THE LEADERSHIP INTERVIEWS.

In developing the initial draft, describe the key events of the future as if they have already occurred. This "affirmation style" of writing is a powerful device for capturing the imagination and commitment of people within the organization.

6. SHARE THE INITIAL DRAFT OF THE DETAILED VISION WITH A REPRESENTATIVE CROSS SECTION OF THE ORGANIZATION—GAIN THEIR FEEDBACK.

7. DEVELOP A SECOND DRAFT OF THE DESCRIPTION BASED ON FEEDBACK GAINED.

8. SHARE THE REVISED VISION WITH THE LEADERSHIP TEAM.

Gain:
  - Commitment to the vision
  - A plan for how to communicate the vision to the rest of the organization
  - A short catch phrase or sentence description that captures the essence of
    the vision

9. ONCE THE VIVID DESCRIPTION OF THE FUTURE IS ESTABLISHED, IMPLICATIONS ARE ASSESSED AND SPECIFIC ACTION PLANS ARE DEVELOPED.

[*]The most definitive work demonstrating the power of an organization vision is the James Collins and Jerry Porras classic, *Built to Last (New York: HarperCollins, 1994)*. In it they show how visionary companies outperform their nonvisionary counterparts over the long haul by a factor of six or more.

same path toward it requires a single point of focus—the *strategic imperative*.

The strategic imperative is *a critical business goal that is highly desirable and presently out of reach, but, when accomplished, will create a significant competitive advantage.* It is the single goal that, when achieved, makes the vision not just possible, but inevitable.

The notion of a single goal, a single point of focus that, when achieved, changes everything about the organization stands in marked contrast to piling on initiative after initiative as the means to improve performance. In fact, the strategic imperative view seems utterly unrealistic—do one thing and change everything else? Yet, systems theory provides us with an explanation of why this can (and does) happen.

Due to the interrelationship of the parts of any large system, a single change in one locale can have a profound effect across the entirety of the system. It's analogous to a line of carefully placed dominoes: The act of pushing over one creates a chain reaction that affects all the others. The single point of change can have a positive effect (such as an increase in exercise leading to systemwide changes in the body that can ultimately increase life expectancy), or a negative one (as with increasing carbon monoxide emissions that can lead to widespread climatic change).

The idea that a single change can have big consequences across an entire organization is not new, but it is not a typical part of the tool kit for managers seeking to transform their organization. It seems too easy, too simplistic. Yet, organizations that have maintained their focus on a single, thought-out strategic imperative have achieved extraordinary results.

Quality as a Strategic Imperative

The C-17 cargo and troop transport is one of the most flexible military aircraft ever produced. It can carry 170,900 pounds of cargo (that's enough capacity for two Abrams battle tanks) on one mission, and then be reconfigured to carry up to 102 paratroopers and all their required equipment on the next. It can land on a gravel runway that's as short as 3,000 feet, turn completely around inside a ninety-foot radius, and then take off in less than 1,800 feet. It can fly 2,400 nautical miles at a speed of 450 knots per hour (Mach .74), and can be refueled in flight—a critical feature that gives the U.S. government the capability to provide aid (whether it be food and medicine, or tanks and weaponry) to virtually any corner of the globe within hours of an international incident.[4] For a modern military focused on fast deployment, it is a critical piece of hardware, but back in 1993, the C-17 was no longer seen as an integral part of military strategy—and not because it wasn't viewed as necessary. The C-17 had become the butt of jokes about wasteful military spending because McDonnell-Douglas couldn't deliver it.

A frustrated Air Force sought to cancel all future orders, leaving the total number of aircraft produced to be no more than forty. From its vantage point, only ever-increasing costs, poor quality, and unreliable delivery dates filled the foreseeable future. The jet transport the Air Force had so desperately wanted—a true technical marvel on the drafting board, and a key component in future military strategy—was an albatross on the manufacturing floor.

Recognizing that the jet transport was about to follow the path of the Spruce Goose, Don Kozlowski, then head of the C-17 program, set out to achieve a performance breakthrough. He set a strategic imperative that called for dramatic improvements in quality. To Kozlowski, quality was the key to eliminating waste in all its forms, including wasted time and material. If quality could be improved, he reasoned, airplane production could go from six a year to twelve a year, without increasing the size of the workforce. The goal, in effect, was a two-time improvement in productivity through substantial quality gains. His rationale was simple: Of all the changes he could introduce, quality was the single point that could most dramatically impact everything else that was wrong with the C-17. With better quality performance come improved processes; improved processes lead to less rework (leading to lower costs and increased productivity); and the less rework, the more predictable the delivery dates (which, Kozlowski correctly reasoned, would lead to improved relations with the U.S. Air Force). In a cause-and-effect tree, quality was the trunk that would lead to multiple branches of success. And it could potentially position the C-17 to increase its business.

Three years later, the cost of the C-17 had decreased by nearly 40 percent, production had doubled to twelve planes per year, and new orders were filing in. In wartime work in Kosovo, the airplane, which comprised less than 27 percent of the airlift capacity, delivered 60 percent of the cargo with a 98 percent dispatch reliability. And, by 1998, the employees at the Long Beach facility were celebrating the winning of the Malcolm Baldrige National Quality Award.

The key in identifying the strategic imperative is to understand the vision of the future with enough clarity that the single point of leverage becomes obvious. In the case of the C-17, that point was quality—dramatic improvements in quality led to decreased cost, improved delivery, greater productivity, heightened morale, and, ultimately, a dramatic expansion of the program and great financial performance for Boeing (after its merger with McDonnell-Douglas). The U.S. Air Force, which once threatened "forty and no more," has taken delivery of over 120 C-17s, and Boeing has another sixty confirmed orders coming its way.

For M. Farooq Kathwari, the president of Ethan Allen Interiors, Inc., the strategic imperative was to modernize the offerings of the American furniture icon. When Kathwari took over Ethan

Allen, some furniture designs had not been updated in over forty years, and many of the company's 300-plus stores appeared more like colonial museums than commercial outlets. Launching a series of new models, coupled with a redesigning of their stores, has helped Ethan Allen achieve the highest profit margins of any furniture manufacturer.[5]

Many change initiatives lose momentum by the sheer weight of their complexity. Managers do not know the best way to allocate the limited resources they have, given the number of changes they are expected to execute. The strategic imperative eliminates the potential for this confusion: It declares the single priority, the one area to focus on above all else. The job of management is to then align the systems and processes within the organization toward achieving it.

The Discipline of a Drumbeat

The achievement of this alignment requires a disciplined process, one that reinforces the new roles, behaviors, and systems that the transformational change needs for success. Nowhere is the required change greater than in the ranks of the leadership team.

Within Naval Aircraft Programs, this disciplined process became known as the *drumbeat calendar.* The word "drumbeat" was used to emphasize that there would be a constant rhythm, a continuous beat, that the leadership team would march to as it worked to transform Naval Aircraft Programs into a customer-intimate, solutions-centered organization. The drumbeat calendar that was developed listed those events that—if executed in a regular, consistent manner by the leadership team—would ensure significant movement toward achieving Naval Aircraft Programs' four-pronged strategic imperative: (1) A positive trajectory of growth (both in revenue and profitability); (2) sustained, predictable performance; (3) positive customer satisfaction; and (4) empowered and engaged employees. The list of events that appeared on the leadership team's calendar was developed to ensure that the elements of leadership, strategic planning, customer and markets, information and analysis, people, and process management were all aligned with the strategic imperative.

The Naval Aircraft Programs drumbeat emphasized a variety of new behaviors, such as regular leadership meetings to review customer feedback and coordinate customer contacts; the creation of a formal process for measuring the level of customer satisfaction; a regular pattern of organization-wide "all hands" meetings to share pertinent information about the organization's new direction; and reviews of core processes, including customer relationship mapping, program management best practices, and contracting and business management. The discipline of the drumbeat ensured that leadership activities would be fully aligned with the Naval Aircraft Programs strategic imperative.

The drumbeat calendar attempts to answer the question, "What do we need to make 'routine' in order for our strategic imperative to be achieved?" The calendar defines the new organizational habits that are required. As these new routines are rhythmically performed to the cadence of the drumbeat, new norms form. The organization begins the process of moving toward its desired future through disciplined repetition.

Embracing Simplicity

Transforming a large organization requires extraordinary focus, clarity, and simplicity. The leader must not forget that people are the actors of change. People will move toward what they can see, what they can understand, what has meaning, relevance, and clarity, and what engages them. They will not move toward obscurity, or complexity that defies simple explanation. This becomes organizational fog.

Shaping the future begins with a clear recognition of the threats and opportunities the organization will face in the future. Once these are understood, the organization's response is described, not in terms of the direction the organization needs to take, but rather the destination it seeks. The desired future is envisioned as if it has already occurred, so that it becomes a place we can see and experience, even before it exists. By creating a picture of the future, we begin to move toward it.

The future destination has a critical few inflexion points—those goals whose achievement is required for completing the journey. The strategic imperative is the most significant of all the inflexion points. It is the single goal whose achievement provides us with the most direct crossing to the future we seek.

The drumbeat calendar helps to ensure that the change becomes routine and habitual. It defines the standard events that the leadership team must attend to, so they can fully demonstrate their support of the transformation. By taking the form of a yearlong calendar, it provides a clear picture of the new practices and events the team must adopt in order to successfully oversee the change. See Figure 4.7 for an overview of these steps.

The steps are simple, logical, and antifog. But, even with a clear view of the future, a specific imperative to achieve it, and a calendar redefining how the leadership team needs to act to support it, any transformation movement will be met with the reflex of resistance. So, our attention must now turn to understanding the nature of resistance, and how to counter it.

FIGURE 4.7

CREATING TRANSFORMATION FOCUS AND DISCIPLINE

SCENARIO PLANS

A clear understanding of the threats and opportunities the organization will likely face in the near-term and long-term time horizons. This includes the pervasive problem within the industry/market the organization participates in, as well as the impact of the emerging megadigm on the organization's business.

A VIVID DESCRIPTION OF A POSSIBLE FUTURE

Provides a description, in written form, of the future showing how the organization will be positioned to achieve competitive advantage, given the scenarios it will face. Written as if it has already been achieved, it creates a sense of how behaviors, systems, relationships, competitive position, and processes will be at a specific point in the future.

STRATEGIC IMPERATIVE

Identifies the single goal that, if successfully achieved, makes the future as it is described in the vivid description not just possible, but inevitable. The strategic imperative is the Achilles' heel of the status quo, the single point of change that will have the greatest impact across the entire system.

DRUMBEAT CALENDAR

A calendar of events that reinforces the required changes through a disciplined, repeatable, easy- to-understand process. It makes what are significant, transformational changes in behavior seem routine.

Notes

1. The phrase "the fog of war" is usually attributed to Prussian General Carl von Clausewitz. The origin of the phrase dates back to the Napoleonic Wars, when the clouds of smoke from the firing cannons created the appearance of fog on the battlefield. Although von Clausewitz never actually uses the term "fog of war" in his classic book *On War*, he describes the essence of it: "War is the realm of uncertainty; three-quarters of the factors on which action is based are wrapped in a fog of greater or lesser uncertainty."

2. Michael Beer, Russel A. Eisenstat, and Bert Sector, "Why Change Programs Don't Produce Change," *Harvard Business Review,* November–December, 1990.

3. Monty Nebinger, "Lockheed Martin Beats Boeing in Joint Strike Fighter Contest," *Forecast International,* October 26, 2001.

4. To view the full capabilities of this extraordinary aircraft see http://www.af.mil/news/factssheets/C_17_Globmaster_III.html for the official United States Air Force fact sheet on the C-17 Globemaster III.

5. Susan Berfield, "Selling Furniture and Tolerance," *Business Week*, October 22, 2001, pp. 68–72.

5

ACTS OF COUNTERRESISTANCE: Unleashing a Change Epidemic

When the Russian Orthodox Church announced a seemingly minor religious reform in the seventeenth century—the use of three fingers in making the sign of the cross instead of two—mass hysteria erupted that ultimately left 20,000 dissenters dead. In one of the most bizarre of historical atrocities, protestors willingly crowded into barns and churches and set them ablaze, literally burning themselves alive, rather than accept the change.[1]

While the resistance to change that modern managers face never reaches such intensity, this extraordinary historical example points out just how strong resistance to any new idea can become. In extreme cases, rational arguments, a well-articulated case for change, or even "change incentives" will do little to reform the dissenters. In fact, it has the potential to simply deepen their resistance.

How can such irrational behavior be explained? Why do people resist change, even when it will ultimately benefit them? The answer, as we noted in Chapter 2, is surprising. Typically, it is not so much the change that generates resistance, but the *withdrawal* from the status quo.

There is a parallel that can be drawn to addiction here. Once a person develops an addiction—whether to drugs, alcohol, or gambling—he changes both physically and psychologically. These changes further increase the likelihood that the person (now an addict) will resist withdrawal—no matter how convincing the argument that his health and physical well-being could be improved by ending his dependence on the "fix."

Withdrawal is critical to ending the addictive pattern, but the addictive pattern itself lessens the chance that this will ever be attempted. It is a reinforcing spiral: The more fixes the addict receives, the more dependent she becomes on getting the next one. And, with each cycle, withdrawal becomes physically and emotionally more difficult.

In his anthropological research, Claude Levi-Strauss noted that, in some cultures, those cursed by a shaman, or witch doctor, would get sick and sometimes die—as if the curse truly possessed magical properties. In the search for a rational explanation, it was initially assumed that those who had been "cursed" had been given some type of poison by the shaman. The poisoning theory didn't pan out, however, since, in many cases, the person who had received the curse had never been in the presence of the shaman, or even had had any direct contact with him. What was happening? Was there truly some sort of magic that defied a rational explanation? Then the pieces began to fit together, and Levi-Strauss realized that what was being observed had an even more remarkable explanation than supernatural power.

The shaman's power was considered so great that, when it became known that he had performed a curse on a specific individual, the entire community immediately began to treat the person in a completely different pattern of behavior. Band members would withdraw from the cursed, avoid speaking to him, not include him in communal activities, and shun him if he dared enter their homes—all actions that reinforced the belief that death would soon come. Eventually, the cursed member accepted his fate, and an otherwise healthy person simply gave up living. The magic of the shaman had nothing to do with poison, witchcraft, or mysticism; it was all about the strength of social norms—norms so strong that forced withdrawal from them could literally bring a person to choose to die.[2]

Addicted to Corporate Culture

A strong corporate culture can also create dependent-like behavior in its employees. People consistently repeat accepted patterns of behavior and receive, in return, their "fix" of promotions, favorable reviews, more flexible work arrangements, and inclusion in critical meetings. This type of dependent behavior can serve a company well by creating a consistent set of values, norms, and approaches. "The HP way," the set of business and people practices established by company cofounders William Hewlett and David Packard over a half century ago, created a consistent approach of treating people with dignity and respect, providing open communication about the state of the business, developing innovative products and processes, and keeping its divisions small and agile. The corporate culture of General Electric (GE), with its emphasis on lifelong education, full participation, and performance, has become the most studied and benchmarked company in the world. Both HP and GE view their work culture, and the corresponding dependent behavior it drives, as the cornerstone of their competitive advantage.

While a strong culture is a common feature in virtually all companies that are successful over the long haul, culture can also serve as a competitive disadvantage—particularly if the dependent behavior the culture reinforces is out of touch with the requirements of the business environment the organization faces. Lou Gerstner discovered this when he took the helm at IBM—a company whose blue-suit culture had helped it achieve success for decades but was, by the 1990s, contributing to the company's demise. Customers had come to view Big Blue as "out of touch" and "arrogant," its hardware expensive, and its PCs unreliable. After overseeing the dramatic transformation of IBM, a transformation that reestablished it not only as a great hardware company, but also as one of the preeminent consulting services companies, Gerstner observed, "I came to see . . . that culture isn't just one aspect of the game—it is the game."[3] Steven Jobs, who returned as Apple's CEO after a twelve-year absence, discovered the company's entrepreneurial hunger had been replaced by the sated complacency of the large profit margins it had enjoyed during the late 1980s and early 1990s. To restore its competitive position—and hopefully salvage what little market share it had left—he sought to recreate the energy and flair of Apple's past. While on Apple's Cupertino campus, Jobs usually wears shorts and a T-shirt. When keynoting the MacWorld conference, he dons a black mock turtleneck and blue jeans. Jobs looks and acts like the entrepreneur who founded Apple nearly thirty years ago while working from his dad's garage. Apple employees have noticed the new spirit (or, perhaps more accurately, the return of the "old spirit"). Jobs has clearly helped to reestablish Apple as a leading high-tech innovator in everything from industrial design to operating system stability.

The Nature of Culture

Culture consists of artifacts (e.g., cubicles or offices, expensive furniture or bare-bones necessities), behaviors (e.g., regular face-to-face meetings or communication through e-mail; formal attire or shorts and T-shirts) and underlying beliefs (e.g., theory X or theory Y, bureaucratic or ad hoc). If you attend a meeting at Wal-Mart's headquarters, you won't see mahogany furniture, or a nice spread of fruit, muffins, yogurt, coffee, and soda awaiting you in the back of the conference room. In fact, if you're in a desperate need for a cup of coffee, your host will likely point you down the hallway to a vending machine. The artifacts you see at its headquarters emphasize a corporate culture built around low cost (see Figure 5.1).

At Microsoft's Redmond campus, nearly every employee has his own office, regardless of position in the hierarchy. The underlying belief is that software developers need a quiet, isolated work area. Despite the fact that most of the company's employees are not software developers, the tradition of "one person, one office" has stuck. From a space utilization standpoint, it's terribly inefficient and costly—using cubicles would enable far more people to be stationed in the same amount of building space. But, like Wal-Mart's emphasis on thrift, Microsoft's emphasis on a quiet workspace is a strong aspect of its culture.

All companies have a culture. It can be seen in the work behaviors that people commonly demonstrate, the way decisions are usually made, the style of management that is practiced, and the way work areas are designed. An employee must either accept (and be changed by) the culture, or deny it (and leave the organization). Over time the employee becomes the culture. The Wal-Mart employee comes to see the value of thrift; the Microsoft employee appreciates the sanctity of a personal office.

The Illogic of Culture

How subtle can this process be? The answer is so subtle that the people in the organization may not even be aware it is happening,

FIGURE 5.1

THE ELEMENTS OF CULTURE

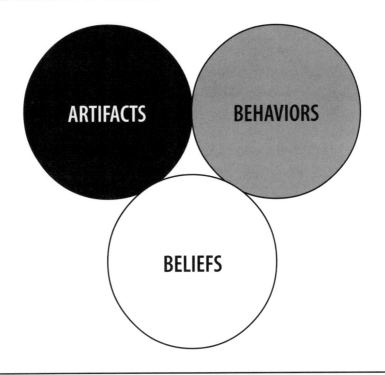

or of the extent of the effect it has on them. In fact, people often come to support cultural norms that lack logic, or rationale. A colleague of ours—we'll call her Anne—was working at a major corporation in the mid-1990s. After a promotion to a director-level position, she was given a new, larger office. Her manager suggested that she decorate her new office in the fashion common within the corporation—with pictures of the company's vast array of products. She was given a catalog from which to order her pictures and frames. After looking through the catalog, she began to wonder what happened to the office pictures of executives who left the company, or retired. After a little research, she discovered that, in fact, there was an entire room filled with hundreds of product pictures, most beautifully framed, from the offices of departing (or transferring) executives. There was even an employee who was in charge of overseeing the "used art collection."

Anne gave the employee a call, asking if she could go into the archive and pick out some pictures. The employee responded, "It is most unusual for someone to want the old stuff."

"But why?" Anne countered. "Some of our products have looked essentially the same for a decade or more. Can I come down and take a look?"

"Oh, sure."

As Anne went into the room, she discovered there was an even bigger selection of photographs and prints than she had seen in the catalog. "What a waste of money always getting a new set every time someone gets promoted," she thought, as she picked out several prints that were to her liking, all in excellent shape.

"These are the ones I'd like to take," she said. The employee responded by asking her what management level she was.

"I'm a director," Anne responded.

"I'm sorry, but a couple of the pictures you've chosen require that you are a vice president. You can't have them," said the employee.

"What do you mean? These pictures are in storage, have been for years, no one is using them, why can't I take them?" replied Anne.

"Because you're not the right level. If someone saw vice president-level pictures in a director's office, and learned you got them here, I would get in big trouble."

What does this little encounter tell you about this organization's "addiction" to hierarchy? Who would you predict drives decisions in this organization—those with the best knowledge, or those with greater position status? Would you guess this organization is "team-based," or bureaucratic?

From this simple story, an entire profile of the organization begins to emerge. The company values its capabilities connected with product development and manufacturing execution (as opposed to, say, "customer intimacy"), hierarchy is well defined and adhered to, perks are viewed as important, and negative consequences are imposed (or, at least there is the perception they are imposed) on those who don't follow the "rules." A transformation effort that runs counter to these well-established norms—to create a work system that encourages high levels of employee involvement and deemphasizes hierarchy and perks, while encouraging knowledge to be the prime driver of decision making—will likely generate significant resistance. The withdrawal from the bureaucratic framework (and its accompanying perks) will simply be too great a leap for many. The very culture of the organization is strongly biased against certain types of change.

Culture as a Change Barrier

The impact of culture as a barrier to change can be illustrated by the logographic script used in Japanese and Chinese written communication. The script—with over 2,000 distinct characters—is very difficult to learn, and very awkward in electronic communication. Written Japanese, which actually incorporates three different types of written characters (hiragana, katakana, and kanji), could be greatly simplified by adopting the Roman alphabet. In fact, the entire Japanese language could be written using just seventeen letters of the Roman alphabet—an economy that rivals the written form of the Hawaiian language (which uses just five vowels and eight consonants).

While there is logic in adopting a simpler, easier-to-use alphabet that would make written communication quicker, the cultural and traditional impact for such a change is far too great for it ever to be seriously contemplated. Imagine the logistics of republishing millions of books, or the impact on tradition by destroying the visual aesthetics of Japanese poetry.[4] The logic of an idea will not lead it toward cultural acceptance.

Even a relatively simple cultural change—such as the transition from the English systems of measures to the metric system—can be fraught with resistance. While the idea of making the transition has been around for at least a hundred years, it has never been successfully executed in the United States. Would adopting the metric system help the United States? The answer is clearly "yes." It would make everything from international trade to following a dessert recipe far simpler. Yet the United States remains one of only about ten nations in the world who are nonmetric. The withdrawal from the old English measures is too much to stomach. As one frustrated prometric congressman summarized during a hearing on conversion back in the 1920s, "According to your theory, [once] a nation adopts a system of some kind, no matter how bad it is, it is better to keep it than go to a new [one]."[5]

It's fair to say that most managers attempting a large-scale change fail to consider the effect the organization's culture will have on their effort. Yet, it is the culture that will either assist the change (because it is consistent with accepted artifacts, behaviors, and beliefs), or greatly work against it (because it's inconsistent with these elements of the culture). Transformational change always affects the culture of the organization, so the greater the cultural bias against the change, the greater the resistance is likely to be.

Herein lies a great irony: The very systems, processes, structures, designs, and values that management has worked hard to reinforce and support through the years may now be among the greatest impediments to transformational change. Even in instances where a new management team arrives with no connection to past practices, and with a mandate to transform the organization, deviation from the past will muster resistance. The cultural addiction has been well cultivated, and logic, rank, and even sheer force of will is often not enough to overcome it.

So how does management begin to overcome the culture of its own creation? How does one overcome history and generations of reinforcing artifacts, behaviors, and beliefs that are out of touch with what is needed for modern success? One beginning point to achieving cultural change is in how managers are "imprinted."

Imprinting a New Culture

Through the years, we have been struck by how executives constantly refer to stories and examples from their distant past—often making connections between present issues and lessons they learned a decade or more earlier. In his research on leadership, Warren Bennis found a similar pattern. Nearly all recognized business leaders had some kind of experience that profoundly shaped how they came to view and practice leadership.[6]

While we all have pivotal moments in our lives, what our observations suggest (and a growing amount of research seems to indicate) is that a finite few key experiences profoundly shape us. Our belief in (or distrust of) people, our views on change, how to most effectively deal with performance problems, and the management philosophy we hold are all shaped by a few key experiences we have had during the course of our career. For most, lifelong learning is not a continuous process. Instead, most of us learn in an episodic fashion. Like Stephen Gould's observations on how evolution occurs, our learning does not proceed in a linear, or gradual, manner; rather, it is punctuated by sudden spikes, and often followed by long complacency periods.

This insight—what we call the tendency toward *episodic learning* (as opposed to *continuous learning*) in adults—is terribly important in understanding how we shape and, ultimately, transform organizational culture. Episodic learning implies that there are teachable moments, instances when the learner is going to be far more receptive to new knowledge and ideas. If we can harness these teachable moments, we can lessen resistance to change by educating it away. Conversely, episodic learning also explains why heavy doses of training about a change initiative don't always yield widespread acceptance—the teachable moment hasn't been activated.

From Ducks to Managers

A teachable moment in an adult learner is loosely analogous to the phenomenon of *imprinting*. Imprinting is a moment when an animal is programmed to receive (and learn) from certain information. The effect of the learning is lifelong, and it cannot be altered or changed later. As an example, the first moving object a duckling sees (upon emerging from the egg) is imprinted as its mother. The duckling will follow this object wherever it goes, always giving it its full attention. In a natural wetlands environment, the first moving object a hatched duckling sees *is* its mother. Being imprinted to her has obvious survival advantages. But, in a laboratory setting, this moment can be manipulated—as Konrad Lorenz did during his early imprinting experiments.[7] The duckling can be imprinted to believe nearly any object is its mother—a human, a potential predator, such as a dog or cat, even a football will work. Once imprinted to an object, the duckling will ignore its natural mother in favor of its artificial one.

For adult learners, there are moments when the learning is most likely to stick—moments when a kind of imprinting can occur that will greatly influence perspectives, methods, even one's underlying management philosophy. But, at what moments in a manager's organizational life does this occur? When is he most receptive to (and most influenced by) new knowledge?

The answer is obvious, if you listen to experienced managers talk about their past. It is almost always *at a point of transition, or change, in their careers.* See Figure 5.2 for examples of "teachable moments." It happens during the first days inside a new company, in the month after their first managerial role, right after a big promotion, inside a team during a major crisis, while on a special assignment in a foreign country. In fact, recent research seems to indicate that most executives—possibly as high as 90 percent—don't have a natural "learning mind-set."[8] In other words, most executives don't reflect on recent events, or current experiences, and develop this into knowledge that they regularly apply. For most, learning seems to occur in fits, at points when there is a transition under way—in the teachable moment.

The Teachable Moment

People, whether consciously or unconsciously, look for guidance when put into an unfamiliar situation, and the first guidance they receive often has a lasting impression. This tendency is so strong that even a random event can impact the conclusions people reach.

FIGURE 5.2

THE TEACHABLE MOMENT

New to the organization

New to position

Promotion

First experience as a project manager

Special, highly important project

When a major threat is facing you that you don't know how to solve

In one study, people were asked to provide estimates of various percentages that they were not likely to know, such as the percentage of African countries in the United Nations. Before giving their answers, the subjects watched as the researcher spun a wheel marked with numbers from one to one hundred. After the wheel stopped on a number, the subjects were then asked to give their estimates. Despite the fact that the number on the wheel was generated entirely at random, it had an effect on the estimates people developed. When the number on the wheel was higher than the correct answer, the subjects' estimates were also higher; when it was lower, so were the estimates of the test subjects.[9]

Benny Suggs, the director of Harley-Davidson University, took advantage of a teachable moment as commanding officer of the *U.S.S. America*. Shortly after he took command of the ship, an accidental boiler explosion aboard resulted in $3 million in damage. Suggs had to weather a lengthy, formal inquiry into the causes of the accident, which was ultimately determined to be a design flaw in the boiler. After the inquiry, Suggs was single-minded in his determination to make this ship—which, historically, had been an average performer—the best in its class. He outlined what he wanted to accomplish to his officers, and then he gave them twenty-four hours to decide if they were with him, or if they would like to be reassigned to a different post—with no questions asked, and favorable recommendations for anyone who chose to leave. "You need to decide," Suggs said, "if you want to run with the big dogs."

None of the officers took the reassignment option, and Suggs, with his new nickname "Big Dog," saw his ship quickly rise to become not only the best in the aircraft carrier class, but the best ship in the entire Atlantic fleet. The teachable moment was sparked by a crisis, but its lesson profoundly affected many of the officers who served with Suggs. Suggs himself views the moment he created as having a lasting impression on him in his new career with Harley-Davidson. "I learned that leadership is best tested in times of adversity. When I'm faced with a challenge now, I know there is a way to not just overcome it, but to use it to strengthen the organization. I don't fear adversity. I welcome it. For once it's overcome, it marks the beginning point of something truly great."

Tom Som, a general manager for The Boeing Company, experienced a teachable moment while serving on an overseas assignment. Som, who had been a plant manager at a Boeing facility in Spokane, Washington, before taking the overseas assignment, was put in charge of starting up a new manufacturing plant in Malaysia. The Malaysian plant, which was to be started from the ground up, was a joint venture between Boeing, Hexel, and two Malaysian partners, Sim Darby and Naluri. Som's mission was twofold: (1)

Get the plant up and running effectively, utilizing the latest technology and management approaches; and (2) transition the ongoing management and operation of the plant to Malaysian managers. As part of his start-up team, Som brought over ten American expatriates (seven from Boeing, three from Hexel), and they all lived in a community together. For Som, the experience was extraordinary. He soon learned that to accomplish his mission, he had to play multiple roles, including liaison to the Malaysian government, principal to the home-schooled children of the expatriates, teacher and mentor to the aspiring Malaysian managers and engineers, community leader responsible for bringing in aspects of American culture (like Super Bowl parties and basketball tournaments) to his fellow Americans, collaborator in bridging the cultural divide between Muslim and Christian views, not to mention manager of a start-up facility. From the experience, Som learned a great deal about acceptance of others, the universal character of people, and the significance of the connection between one's work and personal life.

While the experiences that greatly influenced Suggs and Som weren't carefully crafted as part of a personal development plan, they show the imprinting characteristic of capturing an adult learner in a moment of transition. Now, how do we apply this idea to help transform organizations? We do this by manipulating the moments of transition. *If we carefully craft learning experiences that assist managers at points of transition in their careers, we can begin to transform the culture.*

Cultural Orientation

One obvious transition point occurs when a person joins a company. While most large companies have some form of new employee orientation (NEO), it is usually focused on reviewing medical plan options, how the retirement program works, the number of vacation and sick days the employee will receive—in a word, "administrivia." The deeper, more important issues around company history, vision, values, expectations, stories of corporate heroes—all things that can help to mold the behavior and commitment of the new employee during this most impressionable period—are often nonexistent.

The power of NEO can be profound. To illustrate the point, consider the story of the *Fox* and *Stanley*—two identical U.S. Navy ships. To use the jargon of organization development, the "technical systems" were identical.

Despite being physically identical, differences in their performance had emerged. The *Stanley* was consistently having mechanical problems, and its crew performed poorly during inspections and exercises, while the *Fox* was on its way to becoming the top ship in the class. The performance discrepancy between the ships soon became so great that a perplexed command sent in a team of consultants to examine the management practices of both ships. They wanted to determine the underlying cause of the vast performance difference. Even after complete crew changeovers, the *Fox* consistently performed better than the *Stanley*.

After compiling reams of data through interviews and surveys, the consultants began to get a picture of what led to the discrepancy. To test their observations further, they closely followed two new sailors fresh out of boot camp—one joining the *Fox*, the other the *Stanley*—to compare their personal experiences on the two ships. The findings were startling.

When the test sailor reported to the *Stanley*, he soon discovered that no one had been expecting his arrival. He was asked to wait on the dock while it got sorted out. Two hours later he was asked to come aboard ship and told to go to his compartment—

where there were no available bunks. The sailor was never offered a meal that evening, and he ended up falling asleep on his seabag.

The following day the sailor was paired up with a crew member who was on restriction for drugs (therefore, not granted shore leave). As you might imagine, this orientation to the ship consisted of being told how "messed up" the commanding officer was, how the other officers weren't fair, and how the other enlisted men tended to "rat on one another."

In contrast, the sailor boarding the *Fox* was immediately greeted by the petty officer, who handed him a baseball-style cap with *U.S.S. Fox* embroidered across it. The petty officer explained the winning tradition of the *Fox*, and showed the sailor the many awards that the ship had won during inspections and exercises. Following a tour of the ship, the sailor's role was described, and he was introduced to his immediate officer and the other members of the group that he would be working with. From the moment the new ship member stepped aboard, he felt—the consultants noted—like a member of a winning team.

Of course, there were other factors the consultants identified that also contributed to the huge difference in performance, but it's important to note that among the most significant were those relating to what happened in the first forty-eight hours after a new sailor came aboard ship.

Overcoming the "Peter Principle"

The "Peter Principle" states that managers tend to get promoted to their highest level of incompetence. We can easily recognize this principle at play in corporations, as we observe managers who are "in way over their heads." The Peter Principle is prevalent because many people who are promoted never receive any training, or preparation, for their new jobs. As the teachable moment is lost, the result is predictable: The manager acts pretty much the same way he did before the promotion. While his management approach, knowledge, and skill was adequate a rung or two lower in the hierarchy, he is incompetent in his new position.

Following a promotion, most managers recognize that they have a lot to learn, and they are very open and receptive to learning it. A teachable moment exists. However, the organization's tendency is to dismiss the need for learning at this critical juncture. The attitude is, "If I didn't think you could do the job, I wouldn't have promoted you." In this light, any kind of training or education appears as a vote of no confidence for the newly promoted manager (as if attending any formal training would confirm that the manager wasn't ready for the new role after all). This attitude misses the whole point: Teachable moments are opportunities to shape the future, to take the organization far beyond where it is today by "molding" the next generation of leaders.

Some companies have begun to recognize how critical the period just prior or just following a promotion is, and how receptive most managers are to learning during this episode of personal transition. Boeing, as an example, now requires managers to attend formal training at its Leadership Center in St. Louis, Missouri, following advancements. Through this process Boeing is slowly, steadily increasing the preparedness of its next generation of leaders, and it is evolving a new corporate culture.

The Special Impact of Special Projects

Like a promotion, handling a special project can require a manager to expand her skills and capabilities. Depending on the nature of the project, and how critical its impact is to the business, the experience can be among the most influential in a manager's entire career. Recognizing the power of project management as a means to develop talent, many corporations include "special project" opportunities as a key component of their leadership development process.

When Ed Schaniel took over the C-17 paint shop, the area responsible for covering the mammoth aircraft in a nice coat of gray, there was a host of quality problems frustrating the watchful eye of the Air Force—blotches, dark spots, and splatters were common. Schaniel started to share this quality information with the folks he managed—including the extent of the problems and how the Air Force threatened to take the painting of the planes out of the company's hands altogether. Shortly after the extent of the problem was shared, multimillion-dollar breakthrough ideas emerged from the painters themselves: Monitor the consistency of the incoming paint so that no "bad paint" enters the line, simultaneously working with the vendor to develop a more consistent product, and start using cheap nozzle heads that can be thrown away and replaced after every shift, rather than reusing the expensive ones. After developing tests to check the paint, and making a trip to the local hardware store for nozzles, quality immediately spiked up, and costs shot down.

Schaniel's effectiveness was recognized, and he was given a special project—heading up Employee Involvement (EI) efforts across the C-17 program. Today, he heads up EI efforts across Boeing's entire Integrated Defense Systems organization—in effect, serving as the single person who coordinates and assists company efforts to more effectively utilize the intellectual capabilities of the workforce. Schaniel has developed a great working relationship with the union (Local 148 of the United Aerospace Workers), has learned how to influence upwards, and now sees his efforts slowly developing a new Boeing culture that readily recognizes the inherent value of EI. Further, the experience has made Schaniel one of the greatest advocates, and most experienced practitioners, of EI across the aerospace industry.

The Power of Crisis

Probably the greatest "imprinting" effect on a manager occurs during a crisis. The manager must learn to form a team, work through many issues quickly, and see a solution implemented. Often, crisis situations test not only problem-solving skills and human interaction abilities, but also ethics and personal values.

Nearly twenty years after facing the threat that their company would fold, the managers who led Harley-Davidson through its turnaround still talk about these extraordinary events, and what they personally gained from the experience. Managers at Tektronix's Portable Oscilloscope division—which in 1985 was losing millions, and was on the brink of extinction—still refer to stories from the turnaround in their current management positions. The influence of the impact of crisis can be heard in the voices of the present: Harley's Van Beals continues to stress the importance of controlling costs; former Tektronix General Manager Joe Burger evangelizes the power of lean manufacturing in improving quality, increasing productivity, and lowering cost.

A Long Path to Culture Change

Over the long haul, having consistent new employee orientation and leadership development efforts that are built around teachable moments will clearly strengthen an organization's culture. Puget Sound Energy (PSE), with its new leader development process, is attempting to achieve this very outcome. The intent of its effort is "to create an enduring leadership philosophy, a set of common leadership commitments, and a clear set of leadership practices that generate positive results, and position PSE for a successful future." Through a three-pronged effort built on core training sessions all managers receive, individual development focus through one-on-one coaching, and exposure to leading-edge thinking through an annual leadership conference, PSE hopes to build a stronger, more collaborative work culture.

Efforts like PSE's will likely take years before the culture is fully changed, or altered. So, while capturing the teachable moment and utilizing changes to leadership development practices can help to transform an organization over the long haul, the effort does not yield immediate, short-term results. This requires a more aggressive, much riskier approach.

Epidemic Change

In December 2002 a snake and bird seller from Shunde, China, died of a severe pneumonia. At first, his death didn't attract much notice, but then it was discovered that his wife and several members of the hospital staff who had treated him were suddenly having respiratory problems as well. Days later, a chef, living about a hundred miles to the north in the town of Heyuan, was admitted to a hospital with identical respiratory symptoms. Several new patients followed, further raising suspicions among Chinese doctors that a highly infectious pneumonia of an "unknown agent" had surfaced. Health departments in Shunde, Heyuan, and Zhongshan reported the incidents to Guangdong provincial health authorities.

For the next month, the virus remained largely contained in the Guangdong region until a sixty-year-old lung specialist from Zhongshan #2 Hospital attended the wedding of his nephew in

Hong Kong. Fighting a fever when he arrived, the doctor was carrying what the World Health Organization (WHO) would soon name Severe Acute Respiratory Syndrome (SARS). Highly contagious, the doctor came into contact with two Canadians, an American traveler heading to Hanoi, three women from Singapore, and numerous people living in Hong Kong. Within a month of the wedding, SARS was appearing worldwide—from Malaysia to Canada, from the United States to Vietnam.[10]

The sudden outbreak of this new contagious disease, coupled with the unprecedented pace with which it spread throughout the world, left world health officials in awe. No epidemic had ever been so far reaching so quickly. While the fear of SARS has been greater than its actual impact to date—far more people died from influenza than SARS in 2003—the fact that there is no cure, that it affects the feeble or healthy without discrimination, and that it is easily transmitted from one person to another has experts scrambling to understand it.

The spread of SARS was an international health disaster, and its emergence illustrates the troubling characteristics of an emerging epidemic. Under the right conditions, it can spread so fast, and with such little resistance, that the entire international landscape can be altered within weeks. In addition to the hundreds of deaths attributed to it, the social and economic impact of SARS was also great: Air travel declined, Asian tourism plummeted, businesses were idle, baseball fans stayed home, quarantines were enforced, and schools shut down.

In the case of SARS, a single attendee to a Hong Kong wedding unwittingly caused the spread of a worldwide problem. But could the principles of how an epidemic becomes unleashed be applied to the spread of positive change?[11] Are there lessons here that leaders can apply to create a better future for their organization?

Epidemic Change as a Model for Overcoming Resistance

Classic change management has emphasized the need for "pain" to be present (and widely recognized) before meaningful organizational change can begin. The notion of a "burning platform" has been touted as the centerpiece of good change management. The problem with the felt "pain "approach is twofold: (1) Organizations are often well positioned for the present (even if not well positioned to exploit the future), so there is often no easily identifiable "burning platform" to serve as the rallying point; and (2) emphasizing the pain message, rather than the process of executing change, creates the expectation that, once people see the underlying logic of the change effort, they'll readily accept it—which simply is not true. As we have seen, the persuasive power of company norms and culture can create addictive-like behavior—behavior that may not respond well to logic, or rationale.

The seeming indiscriminate way an epidemic spreads presents a radically different model for how to approach change in organizations. A new body of research—network science—is helping to explain not only how diseases spread worldwide, but also how fashion trends emerge, or why a book moves from obscurity to the top of the best-seller list. Most importantly, network science gives us a starting point for understanding how we can manipulate the formal and informal social linkages within organizations to lessen resistance and create a "prochange" following. See Figure 5.3 for the steps in creating a transformation epidemic.

The Contagion

A flu epidemic begins with a highly contagious virus. What is the "contagion" for beginning an organization transformation? It can be something as simple as a concise, memorable, and interesting

FIGURE 5.3

CREATING A TRANSFORMATION EPIDEMIC

THE EMERGENCE OF AN EPIDEMIC		THE EMERGENCE OF TRANSFORMATIONAL CHANGE
A highly contagious virus appears in an isolated area.	***CONTAGION***	A short, concise, memorable anchoring message is developed that captures the essence of the required transformation.
A few people become infected with the virus.	***CARRIERS***	A critical few people within the organization who strongly support the effort become involved in delivering the message through both formal and informal communication channels.
One (or more) of the carriers has contacts with a large network of people.	***CONNECTORS***	Those well "networked" within the organization (irrespective of their position in the organization hierarchy) are targeted to help build the informal communication channels.
From the new pool of those infected, new connectors emerge, dramatically increasing the spread of the virus.	***CRITICAL MASS***	As the anchoring message spreads within the organization, positive demonstrations of leadership support serve to further strengthen the change.

message that clearly conveys what will be gained by the effort. However, the message must have mind glue—it must stick with the people who hear it the way an advertisement jingle sticks. We refer to this as the *"mind barnacle"* for its characteristic of being memorable and "attaching" itself to people.

The mind barnacle is usually a short summary, containing the essence of the work completed on the strategic visualization and the strategic imperative. In executive summary form, it describes the single point of change the organization needs to pursue. The anchoring message must be easy to understand, and conveyed in less than five minutes. The purpose of the message is to spread the contagion, to get individuals across the organization thinking about the change in a meaningful way.

Following the quality improvements and improved relations with the U.S. Air Force, the mind barnacle message used to take the C-17 program to the next level became "121 and beyond." The slogan eventually appeared on an enormous banner in the manufacturing area. In just three words, a concrete picture of the future emerged: Continue the C-17 production beyond the current 121 Air Force orders. The only way to achieve the goal was to lower cost even further, improve on the Baldrige Quality status, expand the employee involvement efforts, and continue to meet delivery dates. After seeing costs plummet, quality performance improve, and near-perfect delivery dates, the Air Force obliged by pushing the number of C-17s ordered to date to over 180. What's more, there is additional work to develop a commercial version of the aircraft, potentially extending the C-17's life for many more years.

For Joe Wood, president of Famous Footwear, the memorable theme was captured in the acronym IMPACT (Improved Performance and Competitive Transformation). IMPACT encompassed a combination of disciplined inventory management, more effective product allocation at the company's 900 stores, and a streamlining of internal systems and processes.[12]

For Steve Brunner, the manager of a Quaker Oats plant in Danville, Illinois, the mind barnacle at Danville became "Partnership in creating high performance." Brunner, union officer John Pigg, and labor and management representatives worked jointly to plan out and convey this simple but powerful message across the facility.

Carriers and Connectors

Once a clear mind barnacle message has been developed, it must be spread throughout the organization. This is critical. Message carriers must be identified. Initially, this is often a small group of individual supporters who are committed to sharing the message with others. The ideal supporter is well respected, articulate, highly committed to the anchoring message, and in regular contact with an unusually large network of people

It may seem odd that we are emphasizing "messages carriers" with "unusually large networks," rather than large-scale communication events, or large system redesign efforts. The fact is that informal communication channels are almost always more readily believed than formal ones. The things people hear from their peers and bosses in the lunchroom, during a quick elevator conversation, or at the local bar after work are typically given more credence than formal announcements, newsletters, off-site meetings, or global e-mail communiqués. Formal, carefully orchestrated events—while important as part of an overall communication plan—will tend to be viewed with a higher degree of cynicism than communication received through an informal channel, particularly if the workforce has seen other grand change initiatives announced, but never fully implemented, in the past. The "true" motivations of management will be questioned when attending a grand rollout, where the informal chat will tend to be viewed as the "real skinny" on the effort. See Figure 5.4 for a comparison of formal and informal communication channels.

FIGURE 5.4

INFORMAL AND FORMAL CHANNELS OF COMMUNICATION

FORMAL	INFORMAL
Senior management presentations	Chance encounters
Assemblies	Peer-to-peer e-mail
Off-site meetings	Lunchroom conversations
Planned e-mail communications	Parking lot encounters
Most effective at presenting the case for change	Most effective at combating resistance to change
Tend to be viewed as management-biased—only half the "true" story	*Tend to be viewed as the "real story"*

The influencing power of informal communication is a point that is often ignored in large-scale change efforts. (As we noted earlier, the criticality of communication in general is not recognized: The typical change effort is undercommunicated by a factor of ten to one hundred times! In other words, for every necessary hour of communication about the change, there should actually be somewhere between ten to one hundred hours more.[13]) The informal channels of communication appear messy and difficult to predict, and don't seem to follow standard rules when compared to an orchestrated communication event. Yet the fact remains that with the right attention, the informal channels can be focused and utilized as a key communication vehicle for the effort. And information through these channels will be more believed and acted upon than information from nearly any other source.

Within any organization there are social networks—pathways where information readily flows, where decisions are made, where people keep each other informed. Every employee is connected to one or more of these networks, but some employees are connected to many. Debbie Collard is such an employee: She receives and responds to over 130 e-mails a day (we're not talking about spam here—we mean legitimate e-mails from people she knows who are either passing on information to her, or soliciting her advice). In an average day she conducts forty telephone conversations, with another fifty voice mails waiting to be answered. This is not because her job as director of business excellence for Boeing's Aerospace Support requires her to stay connected—it's just her natural way of interacting and keeping in touch with the 2,000-plus people who make up her personal database. On average, she communicates five to six times more each day than her average peer. Collard is a networker—one of the few people in the organization whose network is enormous.

Getting the networkers on board with the change can open the informal communication channels, and it can be a critical supplement to formal communication efforts. In fact, where the formal communication channels are effective at outlining the change, the informal channels are where the resistance to change is best fought.

Well-presented messages in peer-to-peer communication will tend to be taken more seriously (and given more consideration) than any other method.

Willingness to withdraw from the status quo in order to accept a new change is much easier to do if you are part of a group, or team, than if you are acting alone. Communication through the informal networks helps build momentum for the change by demonstrating the breadth of support the transformation has across the organization. The more support that is perceived, the easier the withdrawal from the status quo becomes.

During a two-day work session, in which a design team comprised of labor and management representatives defined the plant's strategic imperative, its anchoring message, and the specific changes that needed to be implemented, the conversation shifted to how to best communicate the work they had accomplished to the other employees at Weyerhaeuser's Drayton Valley, Alberta, sawmill. In fact, nearly 20 percent of the team's time together focused on developing, refining, and practicing the common message they wanted to deliver. The team was planning, in a very systematic way, how to utilize the informal communication network to spread its message.

The reaction within the sawmill to the work developed by the design team was generally favorable. The message, primarily delivered through the informal networks within the mill, was received and accepted. The effort was not seen as a management dictate, but as a truly joint management/labor effort.

Achieving Critical Mass

Through lengthy deliberations, carefully outlining the situation facing the company and how wage concessions were the last available means to keep American Airlines from falling into bankruptcy, Don Carty got the wonderful news—the flight attendants union had followed the same path as the maintenance and pilots union, agreeing to take wage and benefit cuts in order to save the airline. Carty had just overcome an enormous hurdle in maintaining the viability of American Airlines—a hurdle many outside experts thought was insurmountable. With the support from the unions, American now had a chance to transform itself into a more cost-efficient airline. Even some of American's harshest critics were impressed by how well Carty had navigated the company from going into bankruptcy. Yet, less than a week later, the man who had "saved American" was forced to resign.

The story behind Carty's resignation brings up another critical point that is often lost by those leading transformation efforts: *Leadership actions must demonstrate a dramatic commitment to the change.* In Carty's case, many of his actions ran counter to the very change he was attempting to orchestrate. First, there was the retention bonus package for the top six executives who stayed on with the airline through 2005. Under its terms, the executives would receive double their base salary in two payments—one in 2004, the second in 2005. Then there was a "special trust" that protected a portion of the top executives' pension from creditors if the airline went bankrupt. When—just a day after the flight attendants voted to take a significant wage and benefit reduction, amounting to some $340 million—union members learned of the executive bonus package, they felt betrayed, and Carty was seen as untrustworthy and two-faced. All the work that had gone into convincing the unions to take cuts in order to save the airline was nearly lost. In order to restore trust in management, the board of directors was left with little choice but to ask the CEO to step down, leading to Carty's resignation.[14]

At the point where there was widespread acceptance for change, the point where the systems and processes were malleable for transformation, Carty's failure to recognize how union members would perceive the executive compensation and pension package cost him his career, and nearly sent American Airlines into bankruptcy. The resistance to change that had been overcome, the critical mass to support the change that had been achieved, all collapsed when executive actions did not match executive words.

Critical mass is the point in a transformation where there is widespread support and momentum for the change—when the transformation shifts from mild support to pervasive acceptance. Critical mass is the point where the change takes hold and advances occur quickly, easily. The resistance to change disappears as a tsunami of support floods across the organization.

The Five Acts of Counterresistance

Countering resistance to change begins with recognizing the addictive-like quality that organizational norms create. Remember that beginning a transformational change is less about getting people to accept a new idea, and more about getting people to withdraw from the comfort of current patterns. As we noted, most organizational patterns/norms are created—whether knowingly or unknowingly—by the management of the organization. One means to begin changing norms is by educating managers differently. This is best achieved by capturing the teachable moments—those instances when managers will be most receptive to new ideas—and filling the educational sessions with the knowledge and skills that leaders will need in the future. Over time, these managers will begin to shape a new set of artifacts, behaviors, and beliefs that begin to transform the culture. *The first act of counterresistance is to capture the teachable moments, and utilize them as a means to begin transforming the culture.*

Resistance to change can be countered, sometimes before it even surfaces, by applying the principles of an epidemic—in effect, creating a highly contagious "prochange" flu. Like a spreading epidemic, a well-orchestrated change effort has four components: (1) the anchoring message (contagion), (2) the supporters (carriers), (3) the networkers (connectors), and (4) the critical mass (coverage). The second act of counterresistance is to establish the anchoring message—a short, clear, concise mind barnacle that describes why the change is critical, that is easily remembered, and that is easy to deliver through both formal and informal communication channels. The third and fourth acts of counterresistance both relate to how one gets the message heard—initially through a critical few supporters, then through well-connected "networkers," and, finally, by achieving a critical mass of support. The fifth, and final, act of counterresistance is to ensure that leadership actions remain consistent with leadership rhetoric. See Figure 5.5 for a summary of the five acts of counterresistance.

A Final Thought

The Senoi Semai are a nonviolent people. Within Semai society there is no murder. There are no acts of physical aggression. Even quarrels and disputes are exceptionally rare. The entire construct of their culture is built on maintaining harmony and avoiding violence. Yet these same nonviolent people, when serving as troops under British command, were brutal warriors. In their own culture, the Semai were nonviolent, but, when trained and operating under the

FIGURE 5.5

ACTS OF COUNTERRESISTANCE

---

1. Utilize teachable moments to reshape the culture.

2. Establish a contagious transformation message (the mind barnacle or anchoring message).

3. Utilize both formal and informal communication networks to get the message heard.

4. Consciously plan on how to enlist "networkers," and gain their support in dispersing the message through the informal communication channels.

5. Ensure that leadership actions are consistent with leadership rhetoric.

---

rules of the British military, they willingly fought communist insurgence in Malaya. When asked to explain this profound shift in their behavior, Semai soldiers explained that they had become "drunk with blood." [15]

The power of cultural norms and their impact on behavior can be profound. While certainly not as dramatic as the Semai example, IBM's culture is very different today than it was a decade ago. And, a longtime manager within Boeing's C-17 program says, "It's as if we live on a different planet now." In both examples, a new culture has emerged, better suited for the challenges of the future.

Shaping the future requires establishing new cultural norms

that better position the organization for tomorrow. As we have seen, this may require overcoming addictive-like resistance to change by creating a prochange epidemic. But, even as resistance wanes, achieving the strategic imperative may require something more—it may require nothing less than a breakthrough.

Notes

1. Richard A. Barrett, *Culture and Conduct: An Excursion in Anthropology, 2nd Edition* (Belmont, Calif.: Wadsworth Publishing, 1991), p. 82.

2. Claude Levi-Strauss, *Structural Anthropology* (New York: Basic Books, 1958), pp. 167–185.

3. Louis V. Gerstner, *Who Says Elephants Can't Dance? Inside IBM's Historic Turnaround* (New York: HarperCollins, 2002), p. 182.

4. Barrett, pp. 105–113.

5. Ibid., p. 112.

6. Warren G. Bennis and Robert J. Thomas, "The Crucibles of Leadership," *Harvard Business Review,* September 2002.

7. A short description of Lorenz's work can be found in Douglas L. Hintzman, *The Psychology of Learning and Memory* (San Francisco: W.H. Freeman, 1978), p. 174.

8. Anne G. Perkins, "The Learning Mind-set: Who's Got It, What It's Good For," *Harvard Business Review,* March–April 1994, pp. 11–12.

9. Tversky and Kahneman, 1977, cited in Patrick Colm Hogan, *The Culture of Conformism: Understanding Social Consent* (Durham and London: Duke University Press, 2001).

10. Elisabeth Rosenthal (writer for *The New York Times*), "Global Epidemic Grew from Chinese Province," *The Seattle Times,* Nation & World section, April 27, 2003.

11. In his book *The Tipping Point,* Malcolm Gladwell demonstrates how the manner in which an epidemic spreads can be applied to a variety

of social phenomena, from the spread of a fashion to controlling city crime. See Malcolm Gladwell, *The Tipping Point: How Little Things Can Make a Big Difference* (Boston: Little, Brown and Company, 2000).

12. Matt Powell, "Staging a Comeback," *Sporting Goods Business*, February 2003, p. 48.

13. John Kotter, *Leading Change* (Boston: Harvard Business School Press, 1996).

14. For more information on Don Carty's failed turnaround, see Banstetter, Trebor, and Bob Cox (Knight Ridder Newspapers), "Airline's Perks Outrage Unions: Exec Bonuses Revealed After Workers OK Cuts," *The Seattle Times,* Business & Technology section, April 18, 2003; David Koenig (The Associated Press), "Airline Yanks Executive Bonuses," *The Seattle Times,* Business & Technology section, April 19, 2003; David Koenig (The Associated Press), "American Airlines CEO Resigns; Bankruptcy Avoided," *The Seattle Times,* Business & Technology section, April 24, 2003; David Koenig (The Associated Press), "American Wraps Up Labor Deal, Averts Immediate Bankruptcy Filing," *The Seattle Times,* Business & Technology section, April 25, 2003; Sara Kehaulani Goo (*The Washington Post*), "American Airlines Ousts CEO Amid Labor Uproar," *The Seattle Times,* Business & Technology section, April 25, 2003.

15. Robert Knox Dentan, *The Semai: A Nonviolent People of Malaya* (New York: Holt, Rinehart and Winston, 1968), p. 58.

BREAKTHROUGH IN ACTION: Destroying the Box of Complacency

During the last Ice Age, about 30,000 years ago, the hominid species Homo neanderthalensis (more commonly know as Neanderthal man) vanished from the face of the earth. This occurred despite a compact stature and large musculature that provided substantial physical advantage over our own species in the bitter cold climate. Further, fossil evidence indicates Neanderthal's brain was larger than that of its main competitor, Homo sapiens. Yet Neanderthal became extinct, while our species thrived. Why? How did a better-adapted physique and a larger brain lose out?

While the exact cause of Neanderthal's extinction may never be fully known, one of the leading theories speculates that this hominid's lack of symbolic language ultimately led to its demise. Current evidence suggests Neanderthal was unable to develop speech (due to physical limitations of its larynx). The species did not record—through cave drawings, as Homo sapiens did—the world it saw. And, presumably, it did not have the capability to pass

down—except in the most rudimentary ways—significant technological or social advances from one generation to the next.[1] In the
Neanderthal world, a major breakthrough, such as the invention of
a stone tool, or the development of a new ritual, died with the passing of the generation that created it.

The story of Neanderthal's demise highlights two critical characteristics of breakthrough advances: (1) Small or simple changes
can often have enormous systemwide consequences (the Homo sapiens' larynx, a seemingly inconsequential evolutionary development, may have been the key attribute that enabled our species to
survive); and (2) without a means to share the knowledge, and further develop it, the impact of a breakthrough is an isolated event
that has little or no enduring effect (Neanderthal's lack of symbolic
language limited its ability to sustain breakthroughs within its society).

Small Breakthroughs, Enormous Impact

Earlier, we examined how shaping the future requires us to approach many of the issues connected with transformational change
in a seemingly counterintuitive manner. The more complex the required transformation, the greater the need for simplicity in setting
the strategic imperative. The greater the level of resistance to the
change that surfaces during formal meetings, the greater the emphasis needs to be on influencing through informal networks. The more
grandiose the future vision, the greater the need for a down-to-
earth, detailed description of what it will look like.

Breakthrough is paradoxical in much the same way. The simple changes (at least, conceptually simple) often lead to the most
dramatic breakthrough improvements. On the Boeing 747 jumbo

jet production line, a move from a static production process (where the airplanes were parked in a herringbone formation at a production station for days at a time) to a continuously moving line—conceptually, a very simple shift—set up the critical path that led to dramatic cost reductions, significant productivity increases, and better quality performance. Granted, executing the change was wrought with many complexities (e.g., just how do you keep an aircraft that weighs over a half million pounds continuously moving?), but the idea was Henry Ford simple.

As was the case in the 747 production line, the right breakthrough can play a substantial role in transforming the entire system. Boeing first applied the concept of a moving production line to its 717 and 737 aircraft. Using the knowledge gained from that breakthrough, they were able to apply the moving production line to the 747 jumbo jet, and the lessons learned from this further innovation will help generate even greater advances in the manufacture of new aircraft—such as the Boeing 7E7. Boeing recognizes that without the sharing of knowledge, even the most dramatic breakthrough achievements will become little more than isolated events.

Breakthrough Isolationism

Xerox discovered this the hard way. Xerox researchers created a breakthrough operating system built around easy-to-understand icons (rather than word commands). The work came to be seen within the company as interesting, but lacking significant commercial application. While on a tour of their facility, several key Apple employees, including Steven Jobs saw the "mothballed" innovation and immediately recognized that a graphic user interface was the future of computer operating systems. They took the concept back to Apple, received board approval, and began work on what would become the Mac OS—a user-friendly operating system that helped Apple Computer become one of the fastest-growing companies of the 1980s.

In another example, after a twenty-year track record of being the most productive plant in its division, corporate executives of a major consumer products company finally came to recognize that the management system—not the technology—was responsible for the consistently superior plant performance. "Why," the executive team wondered, "did it take us so long to recognize and support this system?" A good question—especially given the fact that the plant's performance had been 30 percent to 40 percent better than any comparable plant for two decades! The plant itself had become an isolated breakthrough, and no "cave drawings" had been made to help transfer the learning to the other plants in the division.

Defining Breakthrough

While breakthrough thinking is sometimes the result of luck or happenstance, it can also be designed, planned for, and implemented. By its very nature of challenging the status quo, it requires a willingness to look outside current convention for new answers, and the future shaper must be willing to part with past assumptions, beliefs, and behaviors in order to achieve it.

In the context of shaping the future, breakthrough can be defined as:

> The creation of new insights, processes, and practices that lead to a step-function performance improvement. Implementing the breakthrough is critical to achieving the strategic imperative, and requires abandoning, or altering, existing organizational patterns.

The vivid description provides us with a view of what the future looks like. The strategic imperative points us toward the single goal that, if achieved, makes that future possible. Breakthrough, then, is our tool for identifying and implementing the changes that are needed for the goal to be achieved. It is a means to overcome the inertia of the existing system, and to develop new performance capabilities.

A breakthrough has five fundamental requirements:

1. A commitment to a clear, concise, and specific goal that describes the required breakthrough

2. A willingness among team members to suspend their own disbelief, since the means to achieve the breakthrough goal may not be initially known

3. A willingness to challenge old assumptions and approaches and explore new possibilities

4. A willingness to quickly test new ideas with minimum resources (known as the "rapid prototyping" and "minimum requirements" rules)

5. An ability to identify when a setback in the effort has occurred so team members can quickly reassess the situation, and determine the best course of action

Commitment to the Goal

The strategic imperative is the single goal that, if achieved, has the greatest impact on the future of the entire enterprise. Focusing on one goal, rather than multiple initiatives, is a central concept of this book—to overcome complexity with simplicity.

Achieving the strategic imperative is inherently difficult. By definition, the means to achieve it are not entirely known at the time it is set. In most instances, accomplishing the strategic imperative requires a breakthrough (possibly even multiple breakthroughs). The existing organization patterns and practices must be rethought and changed, new learning must be developed and utilized, and a new design put in place.

During Boeing's 747 breakthrough work, the strategic imperative was to extend the life of the 747 program. Boeing recognized that 747 sales could be expanded among airlines as well as major cargo companies, if the cost of the aircraft could be lowered. But to achieve a cost reduction, productivity and process breakthroughs were required, including operating the production line in a manner more consistent with lean manufacturing

Ever since the 747 first rolled out of Boeing's Everett, Washington, plant in 1968, the 747 manufacturing process required that the work be performed at various stations. The plane was angle-parked at a station where work was to be performed on it. When all the work for that station was complete, the plane was then moved to the next station. Based on this flow, the final assembly of a 747 took about twenty-four days.[2]

The system had many inefficiencies. Moving the airplane from one build station to the next was all nonproduction time. Operators and engineers spent as much as two hours a day walking between stations to complete their work, gather up tools, and prepare parts for assembly.

In the case of a moving line, where the shell of the aircraft literally enters through a door at one end of the hangar and slowly moves forward until a completed 747 departs through the door at the opposite end, operators and engineers perform their jobs on the moving aircraft. Under the new system, all the tools, parts, and needed materials come to the plane in kits, rather than being housed in discrete locations at various workstations. Lost production time has been greatly reduced, conformance to lean manufacturing practices improved, and the original cost reduction target nearly achieved.

Many of the breakthroughs required to extend the production of the "Queen of the Sky" were brainstormed and prioritized during a four-day, off-site event that brought together the top engineers, production management, union leadership, and representatives from key suppliers (over one hundred people in all). It was readily recognized that, with Airbus's planned A380 super-jumbo jet to soon enter production, competition was about to intensify. And yet, Boeing also had a golden opportunity if it could demonstrate to the airlines and freight companies that it provided a superior value for the money.

One of the fundamental tenets of breakthrough methodology (as it was applied at Boeing) is that knowing how to accomplish a goal is unimportant during the formative stages of the work; believing that the goal can be accomplished, however, is critical to success. Put another way, if we believe and are committed to the accomplishment of the goal, we will ultimately develop the means to achieve it. Breakthrough requires a leap of faith—a commitment to something we believe in and think possible, even when we have no idea how to make it happen.

In this context, commitment is *the unbendable intent to accomplish a goal.* When a person, team, or organization is operating from this level of commitment, new possibilities arise that are hidden to cynics and skeptics. The focus of those who are committed to the goal changes, and they become more aware of opportunities that they formerly ignored, or dismissed. See Figure 6.1 for a summary of how breakthrough was applied within the 747 program.

As one of the 747 production managers put it:

Once we agreed on the moving line concept, improvement ideas started popping up like mad. I had worked

FIGURE 6.1

HOW BOEING DEFINED A BREAKTHROUGH

STRATEGIC IMPERATIVE

Extend the life of the 747 program.

BREAKTHROUGH

To achieve the strategic imperative, create a moving assembly line built on lean manufacturing principles that increase productivity, quality, and efficiency.

IMPLICATIONS

- Rethinking of the entire production process

- New expectations from suppliers

- New expectations from production workers

- Support from union and management

at Boeing my whole career and saw more great ideas
generated as we thought through how to apply the moving line than I had seen over the previous twenty years.
By making a commitment to the moving line, opportunities started appearing from everywhere.

The Commitment Factors

Creating this sense of unbendable intent is achieved when four factors are present:

1. The degree of strategic *relevance* that achieving the goal
   has for the entire organization
2. The depth of *meaning* or perceived importance of the goal,
   both on a personal and team level
3. The degree of *clarity* members have about what will be
   required of them and their team to achieve the goal
4. The degree of direct *involvement* the team has in making
   decisions and executing actions that will impact the
   achievement of the goal (see Figure 6.2)

The relevance of the strategic imperative was created by Geoff
Peace, program manager for the 747, who described projections of
the future showing orders dropping off precipitously. The way to
fight this decline was to enhance the value of the product in the
eyes of the customer. Cost reduction was clearly one of the keys to
shaping a positive future for the jumbo jet. Without such a change,
747 production would be greatly reduced.

The meaning of this for managers and engineers—many of
whom had spent their entire career as part of the 747 program—was
profound. The 747 is the very symbol of Boeing's leadership in

FIGURE 6.2

CREATING COMMITMENT

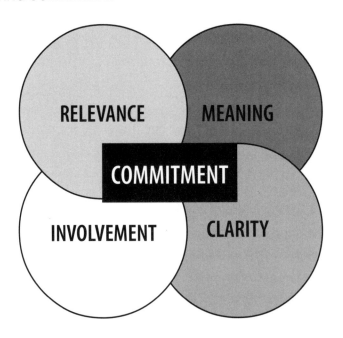

commercial aviation, and it is also a matter of national pride. (The Boeing 747 was depicted on a stamp issued by the U.S. Postal Service, reflecting its importance to the nation, both as an example of American ingenuity and as a significant export.) On a personal level, the success or failure of the cost reduction effort would have a direct impact on the livelihood of thousands in the Puget Sound area of Washington state.

Clarity about how the strategic imperative could be achieved surfaced during the breakthrough session. This is where ideas emerged on how to lower costs, including how to make the transition to the moving production line. Every meeting attendee was impacted by the complete change in production philosophy.

A key to the success of the cost reduction was the ongoing involvement by those who attended the breakthrough session. Not only were the one hundred–plus session attendees involved in developing ideas for how to reduce costs, they also became directly involved in the implementation of the solutions that had been developed.

It was these four factors that led to the organization's strong commitment to the 747 moving line and, ultimately, helped reduce program costs. All attempts at achieving a breakthrough begin with this kind of unbendable commitment to a goal, and the belief that it can be achieved even when the means to do it are not fully known.

In Box, Out of the Box

Within any organization there are accepted assumptions, practices, and patterns that are commonly followed. In breakthrough we call the automatic and effortless use of our patterns *"in-box" thinking*. Our "box" represents the sum of the perceptions, images, and concepts that make up our current worldview. We're able to perceive and understand incoming information only to the extent that we can associate the new information with previously set patterns. See Figure 6.3 for common examples of "in-box" thinking.

The journals of Lewis and Clark provide an example of how accepted patterns can often fool us. While crossing the plains of eastern Montana and seeing the Rocky Mountains in the distance to the west, the members of the expedition were consistently fooled by the vast distance they had yet to cover. The physical size of the land and the proportional height of the Rocky Mountains on the horizon were so different from any other mountain range that they had ever encountered that, when applied to their experience base, they consistently misjudged it.

Our in-box thinking represents our current understanding of

FIGURE 6.3

IN-BOX THINKING

Within organizations, "in-box" thinking limits the ability to come up with breakthrough solutions. Here are some familiar and comfortable "facts" that have limited organizations from creating a new future:

- *This organization has always changed slowly. There's no use in trying to speed things up.*

- *The accounting system won't permit the changes we need to make.*

- *Technical leadership is the only critically important factor to our customers.*

- *Employees don't care about the business and can't really be trusted.*

- *I know this territory, and there are no new sales prospects here.*

- *Management will never allow that kind of change.*

reality. It keeps us safe (don't touch an open flame) and reminds us how to handle common life situations (put on extra clothing when cold). Quick, automatic, and dependable, this kind of thinking is our most powerful tool in handling problems of basic survival, but as Lewis and Clark's "Corps of Discovery" learned, it can also lead us to misjudge situations that are unfamiliar.

When we take a historical look backward across various industries, we can see numerous examples of the limitation in assuming tomorrow is a continuation of the past—that current assumptions and patterns will hold true into the future. We see this kind of "in-box" thinking in General Motors (GM) in the 1970s, when its market share dropped from over 40 percent to barely 30 percent—a loss from which the company has never been able to recover. GM executives badly misjudged the impact of higher gas prices on American car buying habits. Small, more fuel-efficient, less expensive, and higher-quality Japanese cars began to gobble up market share in the 1970s. Stuck "in the box" that Americans liked big cars, and would tolerate higher gas prices, GM's dominant position was lost.

Even great visionaries—people who have profoundly shaped the future of their industries—get it wrong at times. IBM's legendary Thomas Watson once thought the world market for computers would be no more than about thirty machines. Bill Gates believed 640K of computer memory would be plenty to run any software application. To both Watson's and Gates's credit, they were able to adopt a new perspective when presented with new evidence that showed their initial assumptions wrong—they were able to look outside the box and consider other possibilities.

In breakthrough the goal is believed possible, but the means to achieve it are undiscovered. Part of this discovery process is to examine new possibilities—possibilities that challenge existing assumptions and patterns. We seek to move our thinking outside the constraints, limitations, and comfort of current perspectives—to move "out of the box."

To begin looking at problems from a new perspective, we must first view commonly held facts as temporary. Instead of focusing on limitations, judgments, and reasons why we can't achieve the goal, we focus on possibilities and "what if" scenarios. This change in thinking about how the problem is approached has a profound impact.

In the 747 moving line project, for example, a boundary condition was set to establish the new production process with minimal impact on budget. This meant that, wherever possible, the organization would utilize or convert existing equipment, rather than buying new tools or introducing expensive automated systems. With this boundary firmly in their minds, the team responsible for developing the method for keeping the 747 physically moving during the production process came up with a $10,000 solution—millions of dollars less than other approaches that had been previously considered.[3]

The means to develop such ideas requires a suspension of automatic, judgmental responses. At its root, judging is all about pattern matching. When a pattern doesn't match what we already know, it's quickly dismissed. It's like the child who refuses to try a new food at the dinner table. She immediately determines that the food will taste bad, even though she has very little information on which to base the judgment, and remains steadfast in her resolve not to touch it. The unique, truly original idea is sometimes dismissed, before it is even understood.

Sustaining Out-of-the-Box Thinking

To sustain out-of-the-box thinking, judgment must be consciously suspended. This is achieved by focusing on forwarding new ideas through asking questions, rather than immediately judging an idea's validity. Exploratory questions focus on learning more details, surfacing more possibilities, and examining new solutions. The person asking the questions is suspending his judgment, until the idea is understood in more detail. Through the questioning process, the soundness of the idea often becomes clear to everyone in the group, including the person who originally developed it.

The discipline of suspending immediate judgment and utilizing exploratory questions often requires watchful group facilitation, and for many, it feels unnatural. See Figure 6.4 for an example of how exploratory questions can forward ideas. The desire to quickly get to the point supersedes the discipline of first seeking to understand before passing judgement. Discussing ideas that represent significant breaks with current convention are energizing for some, but uncomfortable for others—particularly if the implied changes will affect their organization structure, their power base, or their budget. In such instances the withdrawal response kicks in, and resistance heightens. Without facilitation, there is a natural tendency to avoid the difficult—and often the most critical—issues. It is far better to address the issues of structure, power, and budget head-on, rather than avoid them.

FIGURE 6.4

EXPLORATORY QUESTIONS VS. JUDGMENTAL STATEMENTS

JUDGMENTAL	EXPLORATORY
It wouldn't work. We'd never turn a profit if we offered all that custom stuff.	Wouldn't these extras add a lot to the price? How do you think it could be made financially feasible?

During a breakthrough session focused on reducing overhead at Boeing's St. Louis site, an idea emerged that changed the focus of the organization. For decades, the site had been known as "Fighter Town U.S.A.," due to the legacy of fighter jet platforms that had been built there, including the FH-1 Phantom, F2H Banshee, F3H Demon, F-4C Phantom, F101 VooDoo, AV-8 Harrier, F-15 Eagle, and the F/A-18 Hornet. Now, however, it was in transition. The future was clearly going to be very different. In fact, with Boeing losing the joint strike fighter contract to Lockheed Martin, it was possible that within a decade the St. Louis site would no longer be manufacturing jet fighters. So what was the future of Fighter Town U.S.A.? The answer was to become the Warfighter Solutions Center—a place where the new, network-centric aspects of warfare could be the centerpiece, rather than the jet platforms of the past. What was extraordinary about this idea was that, if properly executed, it could position Boeing as the leader in warfighter networks and systems—a much broader potential market than building jet platforms.

Like any truly out-of-the-box idea, the Warfighter Solutions Center became challenged, as more details about how it would work became clear. Through the breakthrough process, however, the idea did have time to incubate and gain executive support, before it could be dismissed outright. It is now gaining momentum as an important strategy that is helping shape the future of Boeing's Integrated Defense Systems. The Warfighters Solution Center is not so much a physical place as it is a concept of how Boeing's St. Louis site will operate to support its customers.

Rapid Development Cycle

The suspension of judgment and the forwarding of ideas through exploratory questioning can lead to original thinking that alters our view of the possible. The ideas that emerge may be untested, however, and implementing them could pose significant risk—particularly if, in application, the idea fails to provide the benefits that were originally envisioned. (Just because an idea is unique, or original, does not necessarily make it better.) In order to guard against significant expenditures and "bet the company" scenarios, the breakthrough methodology adheres to a specific approach for testing new ideas: Utilize minimum requirements, and conduct rapid prototyping.

"Minimum requirements" means applying the fewest possible resources (e.g., time, budget, head count) to test a concept. "Rapid prototyping" means quickly fashioning a model to test the feasibility of a breakthrough idea on a small scale. The two approaches complement one another, leading to a move from concept to application in the shortest time, with the fewest resources. Often, the means to test the applicability of an idea is as ingenious as the idea itself.

In the 747 project, computer simulations were used to test numerous moving line scenarios before any equipment was moved on the factory floor. Through this analysis, engineers were able to identify the best combination of approaches to maximize productivity, minimize required inventory levels, better streamline work flow, and lessen space requirements.[4]

The combined use of minimum requirements and rapid prototyping creates *rapid cycle development*. In combination, these tools make it easier to ask for and gain permission to move a possibility forward. They allow for new concepts to be tested with minimal risk and disruption. For the team, rapid cycle development helps to win management support, avoid excess time and waste, increase confidence through hands-on learning, and maintain focus on the goal of the effort (see Figure 6.5).

FIGURE 6.5

THE RAPID DEVELOPMENT CYCLE

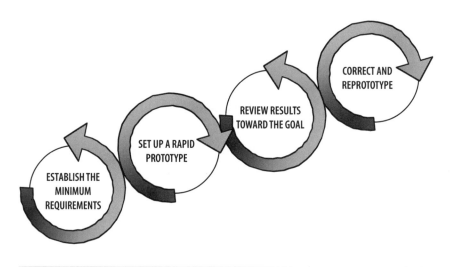

Inevitable Setbacks

Applying rapid cycle development greatly improves the ease with which we can test original ideas. Some ideas do not always work as we anticipate, and they must be quickly discarded, or rethought. Such setbacks are inevitable. They are a by-product of exploring new concepts and approaches. In fact, breakthroughs typically proceed along a jagged path of fits and starts. Progress is made, but then an obstacle arises that wasn't anticipated, and it must be overcome to continue. Achieving a breakthrough requires learning to manage through the many obstacles, problems, and breakdowns that will emerge during the effort.

The causes of setbacks can take on a variety of forms, but among the most common are:

- Lack or withdrawal of support from a critical department, function, or person
- Technical failure
- Shortages of critical materials
- Loss of key team members
- Conflicting goals or time requirements
- An unanticipated consequence of an action that was taken
- Missing a scheduled milestone

The Bureau of Land Management (BLM) encountered (and then overcame) significant setbacks in its efforts to more effectively manage the grazing lands of the American West. Its story illustrates how a setback is sometimes an opportunity to develop a better solution than the one originally applied.[5]

About 40,000 wild horses graze on the public lands of the western United States, and their population increases about 18 percent each year. Since the mustangs compete with cattle for available fodder, ranchers want to limit the growth of the wild herds. Others see the mustang as a part of America's national heritage, and they want to guarantee the continued ability of the wild herds to roam free. Presiding over these often-conflicting views is the BLM.

Under public pressure, Congress passed the Wild Free-Roaming Horse and Burro Act of 1971, which protected the wild herds and appointed the BLM as manager. Then, in 1973, the BLM instituted its Adopt-A-Horse program. As part of its management program, the BLM started capturing (rather than euthanizing) horses to prevent overpopulation of the wild herds. The captured horses could then be adopted for $125 by anyone who had the proper facilities to board horses. The program, which controlled the size of the wild herd without killing horses, was seen as a breakthrough in meeting the concerns of ranchers and those seeking greater protections for the mustangs.

The program, however, had two significant setbacks in the ensuing years. The first surfaced when it became clear that some adopters were using the program strictly for financial gain and defying its very intent of protecting the horses from slaughter. Numerous adopters were paying the $125 fee to get a horse and then quickly sell the animal to a processing plant for $700 or more, pocketing the profit.

The second setback was the unanticipated consequence of having many adopters who had no previous horse-training experience. While providing the animal with a good home, these adopters found the mustangs to be unmanageable without extensive—and expensive—training.

To prevent people from slaughtering animals for profit, the BLM made several changes to their adoption requirements. Under the new requirements, adopters must sign an agreement that states they have "no intent to sell this wild horse . . . for slaughter . . . or processing into commercial products."[6] In addition, adopters are required to care for the horse for a full year, before the federal government grants them ownership of the animal.

The second setback was solved through an innovative program launched jointly by the Colorado Department of Corrections and the BLM. In this program, carefully screened inmates gentle, halter, and saddle train twenty to thirty horses per month. Upon completion of the program, the horses will accept a bit, a saddle, can be ridden, and will load and unload from a horse trailer. The program has the added benefit of serving as therapy for the inmates.[7]

The equine adoption program is not without its critics— ranchers, environmentalists, and animal rights activists all have dif-

fering concerns about how well the program is living up to its
original intent of protecting the wild horses, while ensuring that
healthy range lands are available to livestock.[8] Yet, the program has
clearly been strengthened by changes to the adoption requirements
and by the innovative horse training provided by inmates. Overcoming these setbacks has moved the program closer to achieving
its goals.

Overcoming Setbacks

The key to overcoming a setback is to view it as a means to learn
valuable information that will help strengthen the achievement of
the breakthrough. Setbacks should be viewed as temporary im-
passes—ones that will be overcome. It is critical, however, that
team members describe the nature of a setback as soon as it surfaces and use a logical, disciplined approach to evaluate it.

One of the dynamics that sometimes arises in teams is a hesitancy for members to acknowledge that a setback has actually
occurred, and to admit the severity of its impact on the accomplishment of the team's goal. Team members become so strongly committed to the goal that they come to equate setbacks with failure.
The very reluctance to acknowledge the setback is the reason why
corporations may pour millions of dollars into technologies where
there are no markets, or continue product development efforts
where the technology is simply not feasible. Belief in a future
breakthrough development is so strong that it becomes a con-
straint—a box of unreason is formed where rational thought is replaced with blind faith.

Believing in the future of videodisc technology, RCA poured
millions of dollars into the development of SelectaVision—a pho-
nograph-like system that allowed people to watch movies on their

television sets by playing LP-size discs. While all of its competitors were abandoning the idea of videodiscs in favor of VCRs in the early 1980s, RCA stubbornly held on. Even after a disappointing product launch in 1981, the company continued to fund Selecta-Vision development. In total, an estimated $580 million was spent, supporting the belief that this technology would become as popular as television sets and toasters. Faith overruled logic until 1984, when, after fourteen years of open wallet spending, the setback was finally acknowledged.[9]

The SelectaVision story illustrates why setbacks need to be acknowledged as soon as they occur, the underlying causes defined, and the probable impact of the setback understood. This process must be disciplined and viewed from a rational perspective. If not, the team may be setting up the organization to spend millions of dollars in pursuit of the next Edsel.

Dealing with setbacks is a necessary part of the breakthrough process. The team working on the breakthrough must be committed to the goal, but they must also be rational and disciplined. A defined process for dealing with setbacks must include:

1. Convening the team and acknowledging that there has been a setback.

2. Stating the facts of the setback.

3. Reviewing personal commitments to the breakthrough in light of the setback and deciding on what actions to take, including restructuring, recommitting, or abandonment.

4. Developing an action plan for next steps. (In developing actions and next steps, the team should, again, apply rapid cycle development—minimum requirements and rapid prototyping.)

5. Discussing what was learned from the setback.

The first response is to meet and fully understand the setback. This should take the form of reviewing the present facts and avoiding fixing blame, or dredging through past issues.

When the group has agreement on the nature of the setback, it should then engage in a discussion about what it would take to overcome it. It is useful to challenge the group to use "out-of-the-box" thinking during this discussion.

It is possible that the facets of the setback could cause the group to see the goal as no longer possible, or desirable. Consequently, it is wise to test the group for their continued commitment. Consider questions such as:

- In light of the setback, do you still see this goal as desirable, or possible?
- Are we still committed to achieving the breakthrough?

If the team is still committed to the breakthrough, then it is important to develop a clear action plan so that momentum toward the change can be maintained.

The Breakthrough Discipline

Breakthrough is a disciplined methodology that can help achieve extraordinary results. In shaping the future, leaders must overcome the inertia of the status quo and make changes to systems and processes that enable them to prepare for a new destiny. Breakthroughs—both of a technical and cultural nature—are required during the course of this journey.

Avoiding the Neanderthal fate means a willingness to generate, access, and apply new ideas to complex problems. By identifying

and working on the breakthroughs needed for the strategic imperative to come to fruition, the future shaper is on the pathway of
advancement, and not on the dead end of extinction.

Notes

1. See Ian Tattersall's *Becoming Human: Evolution and Human Uniqueness* (New York: Harvest Books, 1999) for more insights into the evolutionary pathway that ultimately lead to modern man.

2. Roberto F. Lu and Shankar Sundaram. "Manufacturing Process Modeling of Boeing 747 Moving Line Concepts," in E. Yucesan, C.H. Chen, J.L Snowdon, and J.M Charnes, editors, *Proceedings of the 2002 Winter Simulation Conference* (Piscataway, N.J.: IEEE, 2002).

3. Allison Linn (Associated Press), "Boeing Tries a Radical New Concept: The Moving Production Line," *Naples Daily News,* Naples, Florida, April 29, 2002.

4. Ibid.

5. See the BLM Web site for more information on this program at http://www.es.blm.gov/programs/whb/faq.html#2.

6. Ibid.

7. Ibid.

8. For a critical view of the BLM's equine adoption program, see http://www.savewildhorses.org/alliance.htm.

9. Isabelle Royer, "Why Bad Projects Are So Hard to Kill," *Harvard Business Review*, February 2003, pp. 49–50.

A FELLOWSHIP OF CHANGE AGENTS: Building Capability for the Long Haul

Edgar J. Kaufmann, frustrated at Frank Lloyd Wright's apparent lack of progress on the plans for his western Pennsylvania summer house, decided to personally visit the famous architect. He called Wright from Milwaukee, Wisconsin, letting him know that he was on his way to Madison—some 140 miles away—and expected to see a set of plans when he arrived.

Wright, who had been thinking about the design of the house for three months, but who had not yet put anything to paper, sat down at the drafting table and began to work. As other architects and apprentices walked in, they observed his hands flying across the drafting board. The observers began to hand him newly sharpened pencils as soon as the one he was working with became dull so that the phenomenal pace of the work could continue, uninterrupted. It was like watching Mozart or van Gogh—the speed of the work was feverish, and with each pencil stroke, the sheer genius of what he was creating became more apparent. It was a daring, revolutionary design, unlike any other of its day.

Wright finished all the elevation drawings minutes before Kaufmann arrived. A mere three hours had passed from the moment he had sat down at the drafting board to his completion of an entire set of drawings. As he welcomed his client into his office, Wright remarked, "Welcome E.J., we've been waiting for you," and then he presented the design for the house that would become known as Falling Water. Kaufmann was stunned—a great cantilever would suspend the house over a waterfall in a perfect marriage of nature, design, and technology. Today, Falling Water is considered one of the most significant architectural achievements of the twentieth century.[1]

Debates on Frank Lloyd Wright's genius typically center on where to place him in relation to the likes of Bach or Rembrandt. Yet, despite his remarkable accomplishments as an architect, another side of his legacy is equally extraordinary—that of teacher.

With the encouragement of his wife Olgivanna, Frank Lloyd Wright set out to create a school of architecture unlike any other. It was to be a school where interested students would learn about his philosophy of organic architecture by observing nature, building their own shelters, working closely with experienced architects on real client projects, and forming a community where students and architects would meet to share ideas and learn from one another.

The Taliesin Fellowship, as Wright came to call it, emphasized a philosophy of learning by doing. Upon entering the fellowship, apprentice students were paired up with a mentor—an experienced architect who would involve the apprentice in various aspects of her "real work." To learn about the design of kitchens, apprentices were required to prepare meals. To understand the use of masonry, they first had to lay stone. To understand how to interact appropriately with a client, they were required to prepare and participate in black-tie events. There were seminars, often led by Wright himself, to complement the practical experience. The intent was to create both "book smart" and "experience smart" professionals.

The Taliesin Fellowship, which remains a thriving institution to this day, has helped to change the face of architecture and promote Wright's principles of organic design. It has been an enduring force in the ongoing transformation of how people come to perceive (and react to) physical space.

A Fellowship of Support

While there are obvious differences between teaching architecture and teaching business transformation, the model of learning by doing, of developing professionals who are both well educated and well experienced in their subject, and creating a fellowship-like community where ongoing learning and development occur, are all important attributes in sustaining change efforts across large institutions. Many failed efforts, in fact, owe their downfall to the lack of professionals dedicated to facilitating and perpetuating the change.

The power of having a group of internal agents focused on sustaining change efforts first caught our attention at Rockwell-Collins, the electronics company headquartered in Cedar Rapids, Iowa. A number of "high potential" managers and professionals were selected to attend a lengthy workshop intended to develop their change management skills. The original plan was for this group to help consult, facilitate, and support other managers across the company in a kind of internal consulting role upon completion of their training. It soon became evident that the program had a design flaw: Once the managers returned to their "real jobs," they had very little time to provide consulting support to others. So, rather than assisting other managers, the high potentials began applying their newly learned skills on issues within their immediate work area—and with much success. They also began to share knowledge and seek advice from others with whom they had attended the change management class. A kind of informal fellowship evolved, where managers shared knowledge and information about their individual change efforts. Senior management at Rockwell-Collins was so impressed with the results that they began to view the training as an important aspect of management development.

Finding the Middle Ground

In most change efforts there is a tendency to follow one of two extremes when establishing a support system. At one end of the continuum is the tendency to assume the skills and capabilities already reside within the organization—that given the right leadership, the change will happen without the need for a lot of facilitation, support, or development of internal capability. The belief can be stated as: "Change isn't really all that difficult, and it doesn't need a lot of careful planning, facilitation, or processes—we need to just do it."

The other extreme is the assumption that significant change is best led by outsiders—typically external consultants. In this scenario, the organization is largely dependent on the watchful guidance of experts during each phase of the change effort. The underlying belief here is: "We don't know how to do this, so let's bring in the people who do know—we need to let them do it to us."

Ironically both the "just do it" and "let them do it to us" approaches typically fall apart for the same reasons: a lack of meaningful communication throughout the effort, little or no buy-in from key constituents, limited expertise and process knowledge, and ineffective planning for overcoming resistance to change. While the "just do it" school strives for independence from support, the "let them do it" view assumes that dependence on expert support is key. The traps each approach encounters are remarkably similar. The ideal is in the middle ground—where a cadre of employees are trained and developed in tools and techniques for supporting the change, but who reside within the company. In other words, what is needed is the creation of a fellowship of internal change agents whose mission is to support the transformation (see Figure 7.1).

While the organization development function and the strategic planning groups have important roles to play in overseeing various aspects of the change, our experience suggests that a far broader base of support is beneficial, and often critical, to success. We have also come to believe that the best individuals to fill this role, as Rockwell-Collins discovered, are high-potential employees. With high-potentials there are three levels of benefit: (1) It helps address the immediate change issues within the organization; (2) it establishes a cadre of future leaders who are well versed and highly experienced in managing change; and (3) it continues the evolution toward an organizational culture that is accepting and capable of continuous change.

By indoctrinating the most talented into the requirements of successful change management, the very culture of the organization slowly begins to shift. The effort must be formal, engaging, and timed so that it has a lasting imprint on the managers who attend the program. Further, the role the high-potentials play in the transformation effort must be significant and meaningful.

Among the companies that have applied at least some aspect of this approach are Goodyear, IBM Canada, Rockwell-Collins, and

FIGURE 7.1

THE TRANSFORMATION SUPPORT CONTINUUM

INDEPENDENCE	INTERDEPENDENCE	DEPENDENCE
Internal skills and capabilities are believed adequate. *Underlying belief:* Little support is needed to successfully execute the change. *"We need to just do it."*	Internal skills and capabilities can be developed to support the change. *Underlying belief:* A combination of external guidance and the development of internal capability is the best means to ensure that there is adequate, well-trained support through the formation of a "Transformation Fellowship." *"We develop the capability for success over the long haul."*	Internal skills and capabilities are completely lacking. *Underlying belief:* High levels of external, expert support are needed to successfully implement the change because internal capability is so lacking. *"We need to let them do it to us."*

Harley-Davidson. Yet no company, to date, has created a fellowship of change practitioners, all schooled in a common philosophy, who have worked closely with mentor consultants, and who are dedicated to advancing the knowledge utilized in the organization to continuously improve its change capability. Given the pressures of the megadigm and the pervasive problems facing industries, we have concluded that to create an organization capable of shaping its future requires an unparalleled level of internal expertise and knowledge in the art and science of change. A company simply cannot reside on the "just do it" or the "let them do it to us" sides of the continuum and expect to meet these challenges. There is a significant need for developing internal capability that will build and improve over time.

The Characteristics of a Transformation Fellowship

The formation of a fellowship with the capability to support a corporate transformation and ongoing change efforts requires several important characteristics (see Figure 7.2).

A Focused Core Philosophy

The fellowship would apply a specific philosophy of consulting, a specific philosophy of change, and a specific philosophy of organizational purpose and design. In maintaining this sharp focus, the change agents who participate would have a thorough understanding of a common methodology, and be well versed in specific change management tools and techniques.

The power of having change agents with a common vocabulary and a common approach for addressing transformational issues will, by itself, begin to impact the culture of the organization. The intent is not to be dogmatic, but to avoid multiple approaches, models, and philosophies that tend to confuse understanding, rather than deepen it. While all the practitioners would start with a common foundation, it would be expected that, over time, their change methods would evolve and continuously improve.

Action Learning

One of the hallmarks of General Electric's (GE) corporate university in Crotonville is its emphasis on action learning. Many of the

FIGURE 7.2

THE ELEMENTS OF A TRANSFORMATION FELLOWSHIP

A Center for Developing Knowledge

Action Learning

A FELLOWSHIP OF CHANGE AGENTS

A Focused Core Philosophy

Apprentice/Mentor Relationship

university's programs require managers to analyze a problem, or a business opportunity, and then present action plans back to executive leadership. Managers learn how to do market analysis, for example, while working on a real market opportunity. The mission of the university goes beyond educating and developing managers— its work is intertwined in setting corporate direction, resolving pertinent company issues, and developing strategic plans.

The same learning-through-doing methodology is a core element of the educational approach of the fellowship. Participants are quickly engaged in working on real issues whose resolution is critical to the company's change effort. Classroom workshops enhance participant skill and knowledge, but the majority of the work is done in the field under the guidance of a dedicated mentor/teacher.

The Apprentice/Mentor Relationship

Instead of relying solely on a traditional classroom approach, the fellowship is based on a mentoring model. Each participant in the program is guided by a veteran change agent who takes on the role of mentor and works with the apprentice student on actual projects related to major change—both in formal classroom settings and on real organizational issues in the field. Over time, former apprentice students become mentor teachers, working closely in both classroom and field settings to create an ever-broadening base of skilled managers/change agents.

The notion of the apprentice learning from a mentor is a practice that dates back centuries. Today, it remains the cornerstone method for transferring skills and knowledge to aspiring craftsmen and women in many trades. Until the twentieth century, when universities began taking a more dominant role in preparing professionals, it was common to learn a profession by serving first as an apprentice. (This is how Abraham Lincoln learned law and Frank Lloyd Wright learned architecture.) For the apprentice student, the power of being taught theory, and then applying it under the guidance of an experienced mentor, is a powerful learning model, and it is one that modern corporations are well suited to provide.[2]

A Center for Developing Knowledge

The word "fellowship" denotes a community of professionals who share their experiences and ideas to further improve their ability to have a meaningful impact on the organization. After completing their formal training, fellowship members continue to participate in a community of practice where members access and contribute to an ever-growing database of knowledge that contains learning from the change efforts they have been involved in. Participants are expected to take responsibility for the future of the fellowship. Just as they gain from their involvement in the program, so must they also give back to it over time through the ongoing sharing of ideas, observations, direct experiences, and participation as mentors to future apprentice students.

While some members of the fellowship might have a permanent role in assisting and overseeing change efforts across the company—much like an organization development professional—most have core job responsibilities in other areas. Their knowledge of how to lead change becomes applied to the real issues they face, whether they are managers in finance, engineering, manufacturing, human resources, or marketing. Over time, most functional disciplines have leaders with a deep knowledge of change management, enhancing the organization's ability to continually strengthen the shape of its future.

Fellowship members would continually expand their applied knowledge base as their experiences broaden, which, in turn, would lead to the continuous improvement of the methodologies they apply. Thus, the fellowship becomes a place for internal change agents, managers, high-potential employees, and representatives from customers and suppliers to come together and learn how to successfully introduce, implement, and sustain large-scale change efforts. It houses the talent and support necessary to continuously shape the future.

The Impact

While no company has yet fully adopted the approach depicted here, its value in providing the support for major change efforts within a company would be immense, and the lasting impact on the culture of the organization significant. It would lessen dependency on external consultants, while developing leaders well versed in the intricacies of managing change. Whereas creating a cadre of skilled change agents would have seemed an unnecessary luxury ten or fifteen years ago, not having such a capability is a risk today. In an era where change is accelerating, developing change capability throughout the organization is critical to competitive advantage.

Clearly, many of our ideas about how the mechanics of a transformation fellowship would operate need refinement, but we are wholly convinced that the scope of change facing large, complex organizations today is unprecedented, and it will require significant levels of support. The fellowship model is a means to develop change capability from the inside—a formal process that taps into the organization's talent pool and develops skilled change practitioners. Shaping the future is not a one-time event; it is a continual process of defining the next visualization, zeroing in on the next strategic imperative, aligning systems to it, and overcoming the resistance that forms. It requires support, but not from some functional director, group vice president, or even the CEO; it requires support from a collection of the top performers representing all functions across the organization. It requires a fellowship of dedicated change agents.

Notes

1. The story of Frank Lloyd Wright's creation of Falling Water is as remarkable as the great cantilever design that thrusts the house over the top of a waterfall. Wright had sent out apprentice students to the building site to record where every rock, tree, and creek stood on the property. Wright, according to accounts, had memorized all their recordings so that, when he sat down to design Falling Water, he knew how to integrate every feature of the property into his design.

To learn more, see Ken Burns's Public Television special *Frank Lloyd Wright,* 1998. It is readily available in VHS or DVD format.

2. A corporation is an extraordinary learning laboratory. It has the advantage of being self-contained so that the impact of interventions affecting various systems and processes can often be immediately measured and interpreted.

AFTERWORD

Markets shift.

Competitors increase.

Technology disrupts.

Regulations agitate.

So goes the mantra of the modern manager's life. Managers must daily confront challenges that were in the realm of science fiction just a few years ago. Just how do you manage in a world where there is so much disruptive change? A world where your best products, your brilliantly designed business process, or your brand loyalty may be just a couple of years away from obsolescence?

Shaping Tomorrow

Let's take a look at Blockbuster Video, the dominant chain in feeding America's insatiable appetite for home movies, who suddenly finds itself in competition with a five-year-old upstart called Netflix. With an expansive infrastructure that includes over 8,500 store locations and sales of $5 billion, Blockbuster would seem secure as the nation's biggest and—due to its enormous network of stores—most convenient place to rent videos and DVDs.[1] Yet, it's being challenged by a business model that offers even greater convenience, more, titles, and, arguably, a lower cost—and Netflix doesn't have a single store location anywhere. The Netflix advantage comes from an Internet site where customers choose the movies they want to watch from the convenience of their home or office. Customers simply sign up for Netflix for $19.95 a month and check out up to three DVDs of their choice from a list of over 15,000 titles. The DVDs come via U.S. mail with a return, postage-paid envelope that's used to ship the disc back after it's been viewed. Once the viewed disc is returned to Netflix, the next choice on the customer's list is immediately mailed out. The advantages? No late fees, a huge selection, and, to Blockbuster's dismay, no travel to the local video store.

The Netflix business model is so unique that the company has recently received a patent to protect it. Interestingly, it is a model that could only work through the convergence of two other technologies—the widespread use of DVDs in homes (DVD rentals now surpass those of traditional VHS videos) and the acceptance of the Internet as a place to do commerce (the majority of households in the United States today are linked to the Internet). Unlike VHS videotapes, DVDs can be shipped in a one-ounce envelope, making them cheap and easy to mail. Using a Web site as the ordering vehicle, where a subscriber can look up a movie, see what subscribers and critics think about it, and then create a queue of movies for future shipments, has countless advantages over wandering the aisles of a video store.

This example demonstrates the way the future often works: Seemingly unrelated changes lead to the creation of a new business model that may ultimately threaten the market leader. The leader is then left with a bitter choice—hope that the new competitor's approach won't catch on with customers, or transform its own organization to meet the new competition head-on.

For now, Blockbuster is growing at a healthy rate, and it doesn't seem impacted by the emergence of Netflix. The Netflix model is so compelling, though, that it's hard to imagine that it won't soon begin eating away at Blockbuster's market share. And, the scary thing for Blockbuster is that they can't replicate the Netflix approach for fear of patent infringement. It could be that Blockbuster's future is about to be shaped by someone else.

Apple and i

Apple's combination of the iPod music player and its iTunes Web site (where you can download any one of more than 200,000 songs for less than a dollar) has rewritten the distribution rules for the music industry. In fact, Apple's iTunes may serve as the innovation that keeps the music industry, decimated by pirating schemes and its own inability to come up with an easy to use means to distribute music, afloat. With an 8.2 percent decline in United States last year, the industry needed a new approach, one that Apple developed by combining the strengths of its Apple store and its fanaticism for ease of use.[2] One can only imagine the conversations going on at Sony as they read about the millions of customers buying music off the Apple Web site. Has a new path to the future been blazed by Apple Computer? Those in the music industry who are hurriedly attempting to get their own easy-to-use means for downloading music would surely answer, "Yes."

Dell Dreaming

Michael Dell's build-to-order business model, where the product is shipped directly to customers, has dramatically changed how we buy—and the price we pay—for PCs. The Dell direct sales model has lead to a juggernaut that even the merger of Hewlett-Packard and Compaq cannot seem slow. In fact, Dell's sales approach was a strong business model before e-commerce became commonplace; now it seems unstoppable. Go online, read up on the different computer options available, click the exact configuration of hard drive and memory that you want, and wait a few days for it to arrive at your doorstep. How do you gain competitive advantage over such a low-cost manufacturing and distribution system? You can bet many folks at HP are having sleepless nights trying to figure out the answer.

The ability to see the opportunity that exists in synthesizing unrelated advances into a new technology, a unique business model, or a superior management practice is the spark that often leads to the creation of upstarts like Netflix, Dell, or the rebirth of an icon like Apple Computer. It is such innovation that can suddenly redefine the rules for an industry and set the future's course. It is in such a realm that today's leaders must be willing to participate—the realm of future shaper.

The Difference in the Middle

Most of us, of course, don't get the opportunity to set corporate direction, or develop the next innovation that will take the market by storm. Most of us have never even seen the boardroom of the corporation where we work. So, what's our role as shapers of the future? How do the men and women in the middle make a difference? How do we shape tomorrow?

To begin, one of the great myths of change management is that a corporation cannot transform itself without support from the president's office. Many myth believers have seen their grand ideas wither away as they awaited the blessing of the company CEO. The reality is that most corporate innovation comes from the middle ranks, not the executive suites. Those closest to the work, to the customers, to the systems and processes, and to the employees are the ones who see the new opportunities most clearly.

A Landslide of Change

Transforming a division, a plant, a department, or a workgroup to improve its results and upgrade the work lives of its members is important, and critical, work. It is not the scale of what's being transformed that matters, for the small achievements typically create momentum for larger efforts later on. It is the avalanche effect at work: Small successes breed a greater tolerance for risk, a stronger willingness to address resistance, and a clearer picture of what's possible. A critical role for middle managers is dislodging the first stone.

Many managers assume deep change cannot occur until a crisis galvanizes the organization. At the point when the flames of the burning platform are licking at the feet of the management team, the change can finally commence. While the burning platform can help align employees, providing laser-like focus on what needs to be transformed, it is not a prerequisite. Major change can occur during the best of times (as well as the worst). The steps for shaping the future that we've outlined in this book apply whether the organization is on the verge of bankruptcy, or experiencing the best quarter in its history.

A Return of the Entrepreneurial Spirit

Creating a culture capable of continuous change—in good times as well as bad—requires resurrecting the entrepreneurial spirit. Entrepreneurs are filled with vision and possibility; they focus on a single goal that becomes the centerpiece of their efforts; the obstacles they face are seen as temporary; and their mind reverberates with ideas for how to break through the barriers they encounter. Risk is an accepted part of doing business, policy books are skinny, and resources limited, yet there is an enthusiasm that says, "We can change the world." How very different is the spirit and feel of a large, lumbering organization, where hierarchy interferes with experimentation, turf wars are common, and communication flows at a snail's pace. Regain the clarity that comes from a shoestring budget, limited resources, and a big dream about the future. Resurrect the culture the company had in the days when its world headquarters was a garage, where every employee knew who the customers were and cheered when the latest order was shipped. This is the kind of culture that will not just survive upheavals in its marketplace, but will likely create a few upheavals of its own.

A Bureaucratic Tendency

The tendency for many managers is to do the opposite of restoring this spirit—it's to deal with the growing complexity of running a modern organization by layering on more complexity, further distancing employees from customers and executives from the realities of the market. This appears in the complex, multidimensional organization structures, the thousands of highly specialized job descriptions, and the countless change initiatives that are set. In the extreme, so many initiatives are introduced that those managers who are ultimately responsible for their execution fail to support them—not so much out of malice, but out of ignorance. Management time, attention, and energy is so diluted that the twenty, fifty, or one hundred change programs floating around the organization tip managers over the edge of what they can reasonably implement. Their support becomes lackluster, unfocused, or nonexistent. This partly explains why nearly 70 percent of corporate initiatives fail—managers are simply spread too thin, have too little information, or don't understand the big picture. When there are tens (or, in the extreme, hundreds) of priorities vying for attention and resources, there might as well be none. A priority is most meaningful, and will get the most attention and focus and, ultimately, the best chance of success, when it is built around a single goal. The entrepreneur knows this instinctively and focuses her energy on the single opportunity that will create a vital company, but for the bureaucrat there are many silos to be managed, policies to oversee, and politics to be addressed.

To create a culture that links the spirit of the entrepreneur with the tenacity of disciplined execution will require many managers to change many of their deeply ingrained, bureaucratic habits. It is a change that is best, as we discovered through the example of a young equestrian eventer, addressed through a process of unlearning.

A Lesson in Unlearning

"Eventing" consists of three separate disciplines (dressage, cross-country jumping, and stadium jumping) that, in competitions, leads to a single overall score. Both rider and horse must be well-rounded athletes, able to demonstrate the artistry and subtle movement of dressage on one day, the raw speed and daring of cross-country on the next, and the power and grace of stadium jumping on a third. We were pleasantly surprised as we watched a rider compete using a far more advanced style of riding: His seat was more steady, his hands far gentler on the reins, and his posture more upright and relaxed. Later, when we complimented him on his strong performance, he remarked, "I've been engaged in a long process of 'unlearning' past habits. To go forward and have the potential to compete at a higher level, I've had to cleanse my mind from what worked well in the past so that I can fully adopt a new technique for the future."

For many managers, the greatest challenge of their career will be the act of unlearning, of cleansing the mind, of letting go of past success in order to take their organization to a new destination in the future.

In the coming years we will not be reading about transformation artists like Lee Iacocca and Stanley Gault—we will be studying leadership teams who have not just conducted one significant turnaround, but who are involved in redefining and changing their company on a regular basis. One major change may help return you to a competitive position, but, in today's world, the need for reformation does not suddenly go away after one dazzling success. The great companies of tomorrow will be continuously transforming, establishing new markets and patterns that set the standard that others follow.

A Future by Choice

It is easier (and safer) to react to business conditions as they emerge, rather than attempt to define the future. But what is easy rarely enables one to achieve a position of leadership. Whether you seek to be the best company in your industry, or the best team in your function, achieving it requires change. And change requires risk, hard work, and disciplined execution. It also requires leaders who are willing to overcome their own personal fears and unlearn past habits in order to shape their organization's future.

Some view the future as a perilous forest looming before them, a place where many hidden dangers exist. There will be many unknowns in the years ahead, and having a nimble and flexible organization will clearly help to meet these challenges while journeying down the future's dark, uncertain path. But we submit that leaders can go farther; they can blaze the trail toward a better tomorrow.

The future in your industry will be created by someone—why not by you? Why be satisfied with reacting to what others have done, when you can set the agenda that they will follow? The future will happen, but will it happen to you, or because of you? Ultimately, the choice is yours.

Notes

1. Jill Kipnis, "DVD Video Net Rental Takes Off," *Billboard,* August 2, 2003, p.1.
2. Devin Leonard, "Songs in the Key of Steve," *Fortune,* May 12, 2003, pp. 52–62.

INDEX